GUSTO ITALIANO

GUSTO ITALIANO

URSULA FERRIGNO

BAY
BOOKS

SAN FRANCISCO

GUSTO ITALIANO

by Ursula Ferrigno

Copyright © 1999 Octopus Publishing Group Ltd
Text copyright © 1999 by Ursula Ferrigno

First published as *Truly Italian* in Great Britain in 1999 by Mitchell Beazley, an imprint of Octopus Publishing Group Ltd. North American edition published in 2001 by Bay Books, by arrangement with Mitchell Beazley.

Bay Books is an imprint of Bay Books and Tapes, Inc., 555 De Haro St., No. 220, San Francisco, California, 94107.

For the Mitchell Beazley Edition:
Commissioning Editor: Margaret Little
Art Director: Gaye Allen
Editors: Susan Fleming and Margot Richardson
Production: Karen Farquhar
Index: Angie Hipkin

For the Bay Books Edition:
Publisher: James Connolly
Editorial Director: Floyd Yearout
Editor: Karen O'Donnell Stein
Production: Jeff Brandenburg
Printed and Bound by Toppan Printing Company in China.
10 9 8 7 6 5 4 3 2 1

Library of Congress Cataloging-in-Publication Data

Ferrigno, Ursula.
   Gusto italiano : quick and simple vegetarian cooking / Ursula Ferrigno.
      p.   cm.
   Includes index.
   ISBN 1–57959–513–8
   1. Vegetarian cookery. 2. Cookery, Italian. 3. Quick and easy cookery. I. Title.

TX837 .F35 2001
641.5945—dc21   00-068864

Distributed by Publishers Group West

CONTENTS

AN
ITALIAN KITCHEN

WHENEVER I TRAVEL IN ITALY I am surrounded by food, from the colorful, boisterous fruit and vegetable markets and small specialty shops tucked into winding streets, to quiet, reflective places like churches and cathedrals, with paintings such as da Vinci's *Cenacolo* or "Last Supper," depicting a humble meal of bread and wine. Near Siena, at the monastery of Monte Oliveto Maggiore, a beautiful Della Robbia wreath of realistic-looking fruits, vines and flowers welcomes visitors to the serene building and its surrounding landscape. Painted flowers, breads and fruits abound on the walls of the Uffizi Art Gallery in Florence.

I am as enamored of Italian food as the artists were who depicted it so many centuries ago. Like them, I admire its simplicity and its symbolism, and whatever I cook, there is usually a story connecting the dish I am preparing with some aspect of its history. My grandmother, from whom I learned so much about food, used to entertain me for hours with her stories of the families at home in our village of Minori: they were all laden with references to individual anniversaries, to festivals held to mark some part of the religious calendar, or to celebrations to acknowledge the seasonal arrival of one of the local foods.

To learn about Italian food is to understand Italian people – their respect for food and the role it has played in their history. To Italians, food represents more than satisfying hunger: it is the focal point of their lives and their traditions, whether it is *torta pasqualina* (Easter pie made with thirty layers of pastry to commemorate the years of Christ's life), *ossi dei morti* ("bones of the dead" biscuits made in memory of deceased relatives), or a chestnut soup made in autumn with the newly harvested nuts and gilded with a sprinkling of new olive oil, freshly pressed from the abundant fruit. Italian food encapsulates history, tradition and folklore, plus an acute and unique awareness of nature and seasonality, which truly provides "food for thought."

My family comes from the south of Italy, and because our natural daily diet was so rich in the local vegetables, I learned to prefer eating meals that did not include meat. In fact, it is true to say that most Italians eat a diet that is more vegetarian in essence than that of most other nations in Europe. With the accessibility of myriad varieties of pastas, legumes, and rice, and the huge abundance of vegetables and fruit, meat plays a distinctly secondary role in daily life and eating. When it *is* enjoyed, it is usually in quite small quantities, as an afterthought almost: a pasta or fresh vegetable dish is still, to many Italians, the most important intake of the day!

And, of course, because of agricultural tradition, most of the farmland in Italy is given over to vegetable and cereal production rather than to cattle or sheep grazing. And because the majority of this production is small, intimate and organic, with little commerce involved, the farmers are uniquely allied to their land and their produce, with an inherent knowledge of how to nourish the soil and cherish the plants. They sow carefully, grow carefully and harvest carefully, and all this results in what I think are the best vegetables, grains and fruits in the world.

A diet consisting principally of vegetables, grains and fruits, with the addition of seeds and nuts, is an extremely healthy one, attested to by the recent acclamation given to the "Mediterranean Diet" by doctors and other health professionals. Italian food illustrates par excellence the "principles" of this way of eating: an emphasis on carbohydrates such as vegetables, legumes, grains, fruits, seeds and nuts; a lesser intake of protein in the form of meat and dairy products; plus a wide usage of the major unifying factor of the whole of the Mediterranean area: our magnificent olive oil.

The essential elements of diet in general are carbohydrate (and fiber), protein and fat. Carbohydrate, which consists of sugars and starches, is the main fuel of the body, and it is amply supplied in the Italian diet, and in a vegetarian diet. It comes

in two forms, which are generally called "fast-release" and "slow-release." The former are foods such as sugars, cakes, sweets and many refined products, and they give a quick boost to the body's blood sugar levels; these levels soon slump down again, though, which is undesirable. Slow-release or complex carbohydrates give more sustained and valuable energy to the body, as their sugars are, literally, released more slowly into the bloodstream. These foods include vegetables, fruits and grains. You can then understand how a lunch of a vegetable and pasta dish can see you happily through the afternoon. Fiber consists of the parts of vegetables that the human gut cannot digest, and a good intake of it is necessary for an effective metabolism; it is also protective against many diseases.

Amino acids are the building blocks of protein, and many need to be provided in the diet. "Complete" proteins contain all the amino acids necessary for the body, and complete protein foods are meats, dairy products and soybeans (the only one of non-animal origin). Other protein foods are grains, legumes, nuts and seeds, but they do not contain *all* the essential amino acids, so they are known as "incomplete" proteins. However, nature has cleverly arranged that a combination of a complete and incomplete protein – such as egg or cheese with bread, or cheese with pasta, or a grain with legumes and/or nuts (rice with beans, for instance) can provide almost as much necessary protein as expensively reared meat.

Meat also contains a great deal of fat, which is saturated and therefore potentially damaging to the body. We need to have some fat intake, but we should choose in preference polyunsaturated fats, which come from seeds, nuts and grains; vegetarians especially should choose the fats contained in animal by-products such as milk, cheese and eggs. But the supreme health of the peoples who live around the Mediterranean has been directly linked to the glories of olive oil, a monounsaturated fat that actually contributes positively to health. Fat makes food more palatable, and olive oil is the perfect answer.

Also necessary are vitamins and minerals, needed for continuing good health. Fresh raw foods and carefully cooked foods will provide all that you need, and in the *consiglio* – the tip or piece of advice – at the bottom of many recipes, I have pointed out a particular benefit of an ingredient, whether it be the vitamin A contained in yellow pumpkin flesh or the digestive property of fennel seeds.

I have always enjoyed telling students in my cooking classes about the closing of all business activity in Italy between the hours of 1:00 and 4:00 PM. Everyone rushes home to enjoy the main meal of the day; the traffic becomes even more furious than usual and tempers rise as hunger grows. The silent streets thereafter indicate that behind closed doors the very important business of eating, enjoying and unifying the family has begun.

An Italian meal follows a strict pattern and consists of many courses. First, there are *antipasti*, a mere taste of something delicious, or a *minestra*, soup. Then there is the *primo piatto,* the first course, which is pasta, risotto or polenta. The *secondo piatto* is generally the meat or fish course, usually very small, served by itself. This is followed by the *contorno*, vegetable course, then – at least certainly in our family – an *insalata*, or salad. A piece of fresh fruit would be all that most people would have thereafter, or simply a coffee. Cakes and biscuits are for eating with coffee in the morning or afternoon rather than after a meal. Because of this emphasis on foods and dishes following each other rather than being served all at once, the individual flavors of foods and dishes can be so much more recognized and appreciated – one of the aspects I most love about Italian food.

I do urge you to try and eat in this Italian way. It will be a revelation, as I hope this book will be. Although it consists mostly of traditional everyday Italian recipes, none of them requires any special skills, or hours of hard labor in the kitchen (apart from the breads, but that is baking!). They are simple and straightforward, and also extremely colorful, tasty and satisfying. I wish you, your family and all your friends great joy with these dishes.

Ursula Ferrigno

PASTA

Pasta is an ancient food, and cave drawings in Imperia, northern Italy, suggest that it was around long before Marco Polo reportedly brought it from China.

Pasta is fundamental to Italian life; my uncle once said, "A meal without pasta isn't a proper meal." It is a daily ritual, consumed at every lunch or dinner as part of the first course, *primo piatto*, and never as a whole meal on its own. It was once a southern specialty (in the north they favored rice and polenta), but pasta has somehow united Italy, and it is now eaten the length and breadth of the country. During the Renaissance, pasta – especially lasagne, ravioli and tortellini – was found only on the tables of the wealthy. In the nineteenth century, though, it came to be viewed as food for the poor, especially in Naples. This century, Mussolini went so far as to consider banning it from the Italian diet because he thought it made the army lethargic!

Fresh pasta is delicious, if time consuming to make, but most dried pastas are of very good quality and are preferable to the frozen fresh pastas available. I have not given timings in the following recipes, since the package instructions will be more precise: the number of minutes involved will depend on the shape and thickness of the pasta. The pasta is ready when it is tender but with a central resistance to the bite: al dente. Cook the pasta in salted water kept at a rolling boil until done. The sauce you choose will also depend on the pasta's shape and thickness: thin and long pasta suits an oily, more liquid sauce; more complicated shapes will have holes and curves in which a thicker sauce can nestle and cling. In fact, new pastas designed to enhance the "cling" effect are introduced almost as regularly as the new, ever-more-clingy fashions that are modeled on Milan's runways.

Freshly grated Parmesan cheese (the best being Parmigiano Reggiano) is sprinkled on most pasta dishes, enhancing their nutritional benefits with its added protein and calcium. It is not, however, added to most mushroom pasta dishes (nor to fish pastas or risottos).

I eat pasta daily; it's the only thing that I know I will definitely do each day. One's imagination can run riot with ingredients for a pasta sauce: you can use a myriad of vegetables, legumes, cheeses, oils, herbs and spices. Most of the recipes here use the simple pastas – spaghetti and tagliatelle – which are most often used at home, *a casa*, in Italy. This saves having many half-used packages of different shapes cluttering up your cupboards.

I do hope you will enjoy the following selection of my all-time favorite, healthy pasta recipes.

PASTA E FAGIOLI

Pasta and Beans

This famous soup-meal must, according to my grandmother, be served hot with a C shape trickled over the surface in olive oil. Foolishly, I never found out why! The original recipe advises cooking the beans in an earthenware pot in a moderately heated (300°) oven for three hours. I find, however, that excellent results are obtained if the recipe is streamlined and adapted to modern rhythms: cooked and ready to serve in an hour and a half. Italian soups are not as liquid as those elsewhere, so don't worry if it looks too thick.

SERVES 6

1¾ cups (11 ounces) dried cannellini beans, or 2 14-ounce cans cooked beans
1 sprig fresh sage
1 sprig fresh rosemary
2 garlic cloves, peeled and crushed
sea salt and freshly ground black pepper

dried red pepper flakes to taste
7 ounces rigatoni (short, ribbed noodles)
extra virgin olive oil
freshly grated Parmesan to taste

1 Soak the dried beans in water for 24 hours. Drain, cover with fresh water and a lid, and bring to a boil for 10 minutes. Thereafter, add the herbs and garlic and cook over low heat for 40 minutes. If using canned beans, simply drain and rinse, add the herbs and garlic, then just cover with cold water and heat through for about 20 minutes. Top off with more water as necessary.

2 Push the beans and liquid through a sieve to eliminate the tough outer husks, then place the purée in a saucepan. Season with salt and pepper and a pinch of red pepper flakes to taste.

3 Cook the pasta in the bean purée over moderate heat, stirring occasionally to prevent the pasta from sticking. Add a little water, about 4 tablespoons, toward the end of cooking.

4 To serve, drizzle the hot soup with extra virgin olive oil and sprinkle with Parmesan to taste.

A high-carbohydrate and high-energy dish, perfect for winter especially – and it uses virtually no oil. Other legumes could be used in this recipe in place of the cannellini beans. It's so potentially versatile, you'll soon be able to put your own stamp on the recipe.

TAGLIATELLE AL MASCARPONE E SPINACI

Tagliatelle with Mascarpone and Spinach

In Italy, spinach is available in delicatessens, cooked and prepared, squashed and squeezed into a ball ready to take home and dress simply with oil and lemon – the very best way of serving cold cooked vegetables.

SERVES 4

- 2 tablespoons butter
- 1 garlic clove, peeled
- 11 ounces fresh spinach leaves, washed and finely chopped
- ⅔ cup heavy cream
- ⅔ cup (5 ounces) mascarpone cheese
- 10 ounces tagliatelle (ribbon noodles)
- sea salt and freshly ground black pepper
- freshly grated nutmeg

1 Melt the butter, add the whole garlic clove, and cook gently, allowing the garlic to turn golden brown, but taking care not to burn the butter.

2 Add the spinach and cook over low heat until tender, a few minutes only. Remove the garlic.

3 In a separate pan, simmer the cream and mascarpone together gently for a few minutes.

4 Cook the pasta in plenty of boiling salted water until al dente. Drain well and turn into a warm serving bowl.

5 Add first the cream sauce, and then the spinach. Season with salt, pepper and nutmeg to taste and mix well. Serve at once.

Spinach is rich in iron and vitamins A, E and C. It's known as the "international king of vegetables" and is said to prevent many ailments. I particularly love young tender spinach leaves, especially raw in a salad.

TAGLIATELLE AI CARCIOFI

Tagliatelle with Artichokes

Mint and artichokes are great in combination, having a natural affinity with each other. This is a good recipe to treat yourself to during artichoke season, which occurs in the spring and fall.

SERVES 4

4 globe artichokes

2 tablespoons olive oil

2 tablespoons unsalted butter

1 small onion, peeled
  and chopped

⅔ cup dry white wine

juice of 1 lemon

⅔ cup Vegetable Stock
  (page 61)

10 ounces tagliatelle
  (ribbon noodles)

1 cup heavy cream

a handful of fresh mint,
  chopped

sea salt and freshly ground
  black pepper

2 ounces Parmesan, freshly
  grated

1 Prepare the artichokes by removing the tough outer leaves, and cutting off the spiky, pointed top. Remove the stalk and cut each vegetable lengthwise into 8 segments. Cut away the prickly choke and discard any tough leaves that might spoil the sauce. Put the artichoke segments into water with a little vinegar or extra lemon juice to prevent discoloration. Just before using them, drain and chop.

2 Heat the oil and butter in a large saucepan, and gently sauté the chopped onion until soft. Keep the heat low and cover the pan. After about 5 minutes add the chopped artichoke. Stir, cover again and cook for another

5 minutes. Add the white wine, lemon juice and stock. Cook gently, covered, for 15 minutes.

3 Meanwhile, heat the water for the pasta. Once you have added the pasta to the boiling, salted water, stir the cream and mint into the artichoke mixture and leave uncovered over a very low heat. Season with salt and pepper. The sauce will become thick while the pasta is cooking.

4 Drain the pasta when it is al dente, transfer it to a warm serving dish and immediately stir in the freshly grated Parmesan so that all the pasta is coated with the cheese. Now pour on the artichoke sauce and stir vigorously. Serve at once.

Artichokes contain cynarin, an enzyme that is said to be liver protective, to be good for the kidneys and to lower blood cholesterol. Cynarin also makes everything in your mouth taste quite sweet, so you should never try to drink a good wine with artichokes.

TAGLIATELLE ALLA BOSCAIOLA

Tagliatelle "of the Forest"

Italians love wild mushrooms, which grow all over the country in damp, cool forests. The most common wild mushroom is the porcino or cèpe (*Boletus edulis*). It is often dried, which makes the flavor intensify and deepen. You can replace half the mushrooms here with 2 ounces dried porcini: soak them in cold water first for about 10 minutes.

SERVES 4

3 tablespoons olive oil

2 garlic cloves, peeled and
   finely chopped

14 ounces canned or fresh plum
   tomatoes, skinned

sea salt and freshly ground
   black pepper

10 ounces fresh edible wild or
   field mushrooms, wiped
   and finely diced

a handful of fresh flat-leaf
   parsley, chopped

10 ounces tagliatelle
   (ribbon noodles)

1 Heat 2 tablespoons of the olive oil in a sauté pan and add the finely chopped garlic. When it begins to color, add the tomatoes along with their juices, if using canned, and squash them. Add some salt and pepper, and cook briskly for 15 minutes.

2 Meanwhile heat the rest of the oil in a separate sauté pan, and add the mushrooms. Lightly salt, and let them cook gently for 5 minutes. Add the chopped parsley; keep the mixture warm.

3 Cook the pasta in boiling, salted water until al dente. Drain and turn into a heated serving dish. Add the tomato sauce, stirring thoroughly, and then the mushrooms. Stir well and serve at once.

Mushrooms contain a little protein but almost no fat; they are a good source of riboflavin, vitamin B$_2$. This is important for brain function, and it is also linked to the proper absorption of iron. Take extra care to use only mushrooms that are bought in the market or that are proven to be safe to eat; certain wild mushrooms are deadly poisonous.

PASTA E PISELLI

Pasta and Peas

Italians love the pea season in June, and in order to enjoy tender young peas they have developed many, many pea recipes, one of the most famous being *Risi e Bisi* (see page 73). This recipe here is one of my pasta and pea favorites, a great dish for a family since peas seem to be so popular with children.

SERVES 4

1 onion, chopped

4 tablespoons best-quality
   olive oil

2 garlic cloves, peeled

1½ pounds peas in the pod,
   shelled

10 ounces spaghetti

sea salt and freshly ground
   black pepper

a handful of fresh mint,
   finely chopped

freshly grated Parmesan
   to taste (optional)

1 In a medium saucepan gently sauté the onion in the olive oil. When the onion is softened, add the garlic and gently stir to coat in oil.

2 Now add all the peas, and mix well to coat them with oil. Add 3 tablespoons water, place the lid on the pan, and very gently cook for 7 minutes.

3 Meanwhile cook the pasta in boiling, salted water until al dente, then drain and transfer to a warm serving dish.

4 Add the pea sauce to the pasta and toss with plenty of salt and pepper, the mint and the Parmesan, if desired. Serve at once.

Peas, being the seeds of the plant, are extremely rich in nutrients, among them vitamins A, B, C and E, and many minerals. They contain soluble fiber, can help control blood sugar, and may help to lower blood pressure. In folk medicine, the pea's primary claim to fame is as an antifertility agent, and this has been echoed by several conventional medical studies.

TAGLIATELLE AGLI ASPARAGI
Tagliatelle with Asparagus

There are many varieties of asparagus, so do experiment with this particular sauce. All varieties will work well, but I especially like the very thin green stalks that are tender and sweet, known as *selvatica* or "wild" asparagus in Italy. Using green and yellow tagliatelle together – what the Italians call *paglia e fieno*, "straw and hay" – makes the dish look very pretty.

SERVES 4

1 pound asparagus
sea salt
½ cup unsalted butter
1 slice stale white bread,
   made into large crumbs
¾ cup heavy cream
freshly ground black pepper
10 ounces mixed green
   and yellow tagliatelle
   (ribbon noodles)

2 ounces fontina cheese,
   grated
a handful of fresh basil, torn
a handful of fresh flat-leaf
   parsley, finely chopped
freshly grated Parmesan
   to taste (optional)

1 Wash the asparagus, and remove any tough base stalks. Place in a large shallow pan with a lid, add a pinch of sea salt and cover with boiling water. Cook for about 8 minutes: this will depend on the size of the asparagus, so do use your judgment. Drain and plunge into cold water to stop the cooking. Drain again, and cut into ¾-inch lengths, discarding any tough parts.

2 Melt the butter in a large pan, add the bread crumbs, and cook gently, stirring continuously, for about 2 minutes. Now add the cream. Stir well, then add the asparagus and some black pepper to taste. Cook for 5 minutes, then keep warm.

3 Cook the pasta in plenty of boiling, salted water until al dente. Drain, transfer to a warm serving dish and add the asparagus sauce. Add the fontina cheese, basil and parsley, and mix well.

4 Check and adjust the seasoning, and serve at once, with Parmesan, if desired.

Asparagus is a natural blood cleanser due to its vitamin A content. The vitamin B it contains is good for nervous disorders. Spring is the natural season for the vegetable, so make sure you enjoy this dish often at that time!

PAPPARDELLE DELLE COLLINE DI FIRENZE

Pappardelle from the Hills of Florence

Sheep's-milk ricotta cheese may be hard to find, but a good deli may be able to get it for you. Ordinary ricotta, made from pasteurized cow's milk, will happily substitute. We make our own ricotta at the school, from goat's milk.

SERVES 4

- 2 tablespoons olive oil
- 1 onion, peeled and chopped
- 1 carrot, peeled and chopped
- 1 celery stalk, chopped
- 1 garlic clove, peeled and crushed
- 1 cup tomato passata (strained tomatoes)
- ⅔ cup white wine
- sea salt and freshly ground black pepper
- 10 ounces pappardelle (wide ribbon noodles)
- 7 ounces fresh sheep's-milk ricotta cheese
- a handful of fresh basil, torn
- freshly grated Parmesan to taste

1 Heat the oil in a medium saucepan and add the onion, carrot and celery; stir well and cook gently until they soften.

2 Add the garlic, tomato passata, wine, salt and pepper; lower the heat and simmer for 25 minutes, covered. Stir occasionally.

3 Meanwhile, boil the pasta in plenty of boiling, salted water until al dente, then drain.

4 Spoon or crumble the ricotta into a tureen, then pour the hot pasta, the sauce and the basil over the ricotta and mix well. Serve with plenty of Parmesan and garnish with more basil if desired.

Because it is a whey cheese, ricotta is very light and highly digestible – good for those who have stomach problems or who are unwell. I call ricotta a "pantry ingredient," since I can find so many uses for it. Passata is tomato that has been chopped and sieved, leaving behind the seeds.

TAGLIATELLE CON CIPOLLE

Tagliatelle with Onion Sauce

Experiment with the many different types of onion available. Red onions from Tropea, in Calabria, are delicious because the soil is so good. You could use white onions instead, which have a very good flavor, or a combination of the two. Simple, satisfying and surprisingly good.

SERVES 4

½ cup unsalted butter
1 pound onions, peeled
 and thinly sliced
⅔ cup heavy cream
sea salt and freshly ground
 black pepper
a large pinch of freshly
 grated nutmeg

a handful of fresh flat-leaf
 parsley, finely chopped
10 ounces tagliatelle
 (ribbon noodles)
freshly grated Parmesan
 to taste

1 Melt the butter and cook the onion in a covered pan over low heat until the onion is soft. Do not let the onion turn brown. Add a little water, approximately 4 tablespoons, and gently simmer, covered, for 20 minutes.

2 In a food processor, purée the cooked onion, then add the cream, salt, pepper, nutmeg and parsley. Return the onion purée to the pan and keep warm.

3 Cook the pasta in boiling, salted water until al dente, then drain and toss into the sauce. Mix very well, and serve with freshly grated Parmesan.

Onions have antiseptic properties and aid digestion; the cream and cheese both add protein to the dish.

SPAGHETTI ALLA NAPOLETANA

Spaghetti with Tomato and Basil Sauce

There are many different recipes for tomato sauce – including several in this chapter – but this is my grandmother's basic one. Naples is famous for its tomatoes, particularly the San Marzano, which is known as the "true" Italian plum tomato. It is different from the others in shape and flavor: it has "shoulders," and a drier but sweeter flesh. This is also the tomato most commonly dried in the hot southern sun.

SERVES 4

3 tablespoons best-quality
   olive oil
1 onion, peeled and chopped
1¾ pounds ripe tomatoes,
   roughly chopped
sea salt and freshly ground
   black pepper

10 ounces spaghetti
a handful of fresh basil, torn
2 tablespoons chilled unsalted
   butter, cut into pieces
freshly grated Parmesan
   to taste

1 Heat the oil in a heavy pan, add the onion and sauté gently for 5 minutes. Add the tomatoes, and some salt and pepper. Cook gently, covered, for 20 minutes.

2 Meanwhile, cook the spaghetti in plenty of boiling, salted water until al dente, then drain thoroughly.

3 Add the pasta to the tomato sauce and mix. Add the basil and the butter, and toss well. Serve at once with freshly grated Parmesan.

Two types of basil are readily available in Italy: the lattugha *and the* Genovese. *The latter is used for making pesto and has smaller, more flavorful leaves; the former has larger, slightly coarse leaves, which are used for tearing and adding to a dish at the last minute.*

28

SPAGHETTI CON POMODORI E RUCOLA

Spaghetti with Fresh Tomatoes and Arugula

Try to buy wild arugula that has large, pungent leaves. You may be able to find large bundles in gourmet grocery stores and farmers' markets. Some supermarkets sell tiny bags of French arugula, which I think is not so flavorful (and the bags are very expensive).

SERVES 4

10 ounces red, ripe plum
   tomatoes
2 garlic cloves, peeled and
   finely chopped
3½ ounces arugula, coarsely
   chopped
zest of 1 unwaxed lemon,
   grated

1½ tablespoons good-quality
   olive oil
sea salt and freshly ground
   black pepper
10 ounces spaghetti
freshly grated Parmesan
   to taste (optional)

1 To skin the tomatoes, plunge them into boiling water for 20 seconds, then plunge them into very cold water, and slip off the skins. Finely chop the flesh.

2 Place the chopped tomato in a large bowl together with the garlic, arugula, lemon zest, oil, salt and pepper. Let stand for a minimum of 30 minutes.

3 Cook the pasta in plenty of boiling, salted water until al dente, then drain well and transfer to a heated serving dish.

4 Stir the sauce into the pasta. Serve at once, with Parmesan if desired.

A couple of tomato plants in a growing bag, sturdy window box or even a pot can yield an amazing quantity of fruit in late summer. When freshly plucked they are bursting with flavor and nutrients, particularly vitamins A and C.

PASTA AL CARTOCCIO

Spaghetti Baked in Parchment Paper

This is a dish for maximum visual effect. It is perfect for a dinner party, since the flavors and aromas are trapped inside the parchment paper, released only when the paper is slashed open. It's also good for a picnic or lunch in the garden; pasta cools down very quickly after being drained and tossed in its sauce, but wrapped in its paper packaging, it remains wonderfully hot. And parcels always produce a great element of surprise!

SERVES 4

2 tablespoons olive oil

1 large garlic clove, peeled

1 pound ripe fresh tomatoes, chopped

sea salt and freshly ground black pepper

1 teaspoon chopped fresh hot red chile pepper

(peperoncino), de-seeded

10 ounces spaghetti

10 black olives, pitted

a handful of fresh flat-leaf parsley, chopped

freshly grated Parmesan to taste

1 Preheat the oven to 400°. Cut out four pieces of parchment paper, each about 12 x 8 inches.

2 Heat the oil in a saucepan over medium heat; when warm, add the whole garlic clove and sauté for 2 minutes.

3 Discard the garlic, add the chopped tomato to the flavored oil in the pan and simmer for 20 minutes, stirring occasionally with a wooden spoon. Season with salt and pepper and add the chile. Pass the contents of the pan through a food mill. Return to the pan and reduce over medium heat for 10 minutes.

4 Meanwhile cook the pasta in boiling, salted water for half the time indicated on the package only, then drain well.

5 Add the olives and half the parsley to the tomato sauce, then add the pasta and mix. Add more salt and pepper if necessary. Place a portion of pasta in the middle of each piece of parchment paper, and scrunch the edges of each package to tightly close it. Place the packages in a roasting pan and bake for approximately 7 minutes, depending on the thickness of the spaghetti you have chosen.

6 Remove the pan from the oven, and place each package on a warm plate. Guests open their own packages and sprinkle the insides with the remaining parsley leaves and some Parmesan.

I always use flat-leaf parsley because it is easier to clean and chop, and because it just tastes better than curly. Parsley is full of iron and is a stimulant for the liver, something the Italians are obsessed with and talk about on a daily basis!

SPAGHETTI ALLA NORCINA

Spaghetti with Truffles or Mushrooms

Truffles are synonymous with Italy. The white Alba truffle is the principal prize in Piedmont. To sniff them out, dogs are specially trained using cheese scented with truffles. Black truffles from Norcia, in Umbria, are not as highly prized, but in my opinion have more flavor. Winter truffles, *d'inverno*, have more flavor than those of the summer, *l'estate*.

SERVES 4

2 tablespoons olive oil

1 black truffle, sliced, or
  2 ounces dried porcini,
  reconstituted (see below)

1 garlic clove, peeled and
  crushed

a handful of fresh flat-leaf
  parsley, chopped

sea salt and freshly ground
  black pepper

10 ounces spaghetti

a handful of fresh basil,
  finely torn

freshly grated Parmesan
  to taste

1 Heat the oil in a heavy pan, add the truffle or drained porcini, and cook gently for 5 minutes. Remove from the heat and add the garlic and parsley. Return to the heat and cook gently for a few more minutes. Season to taste with salt and pepper.

2 Cook the spaghetti in plenty of boiling, salted water until al dente. Drain thoroughly, then pile into a warm serving dish.

3 Pour the sauce over the spaghetti, mix well, then sprinkle the basil leaves over the top. Serve with plenty of Parmesan.

To reconstitute dried porcini, always use cold water so as not to draw out too much flavor from the mushrooms themselves. Use a minimum quantity of water for the same reason. Cover the mushrooms with water in a bowl and leave for 10 minutes. Pick them out of the water rather than strain them through a sieve (thus leaving any grit in the bowl). You could use the strained soaking water as stock in another dish.

SPAGHETTI VESUVIO

Spaghetti with Vesuvius Sauce

The volcano Vesuvius is near Naples, which is where I first ate this dish. In fact, I was eating it and looking at the gently steaming volcano at the same time!

SERVES 4

1 tablespoon olive oil

14 ounces canned or fresh
plum tomatoes, skinned
and chopped

1 garlic clove, peeled and
crushed

1 teaspoon dried oregano

sea salt and freshly ground
black pepper

10 ounces spaghetti

7 ounces mozzarella
cheese, diced

2 ounces Parmesan,
freshly grated

1 Warm the oil very gently in a pan, and add the tomatoes, along with their juices, if using canned, and the garlic. Stir in the oregano, salt and pepper, and cook rapidly for 20 minutes.

2 While the sauce is cooking, cook the pasta in boiling, salted water until al dente, then drain well. Transfer pasta to a heated, covered serving dish.

3 Add the tomato sauce and the diced mozzarella to the pasta. Toss rapidly, then cover and leave for about 2 minutes so that the mozzarella begins to melt and look like streams of molten lava.

4 Serve at once, with the Parmesan sprinkled on top.

Italians preserve their own fresh tomatoes when there is a glut. When they run out, though, they always seem to go for cans of tomatoes, rather than cartons. These are better value and have a much better flavor. We should never be too disparaging about canned tomatoes: canning is an ancient, but entirely reliable, method of preserving, and the tomatoes used are of the best possible quality and freshness.

TORTELLI DI PATATE

Potato Tortelli

This recipe is dedicated to my father, a great potato lover and grower. You might find the combination of pasta and potato strange, but I promise you that you'll be pleased with the result. Despite consisting of two types of carbohydrate, the tortelli are surprisingly light.

SERVES 6

Pasta

2⅔ cups Italian "00" (soft wheat) or cake (not self-rising) flour

2⅔ cups fine semolina flour

2 teaspoons sea salt

5 eggs

1 tablespoon olive oil

Filling

1¼ pounds russet potatoes, scrubbed

3½ ounces Parmesan, freshly grated

2 garlic cloves, peeled and chopped

a handful of fresh flat-leaf parsley, chopped

4 ripe tomatoes, skinned and diced

½ teaspoon freshly grated nutmeg

sea salt and freshly ground black pepper

1 egg, lightly beaten

To serve

freshly grated Parmesan to taste

1 To make the pasta, heap the flour and semolina into a mound on the work surface. Sprinkle the salt over the mound and mix well. Hollow out a well in the center into which you break the eggs. Add the oil and, with much care and patience, gradually work the eggs and oil into the flour until you have a slab of dough. Shape this into a ball and leave it under a dishcloth to rest while you prepare the filling.

2 To make the filling, boil the potatoes in their skins until tender, then drain, peel and mash. Mix in the remaining ingredients, apart from the egg, adding salt and pepper to taste. Last of all, mix in the egg.

3 Roll out the pasta dough wafer thin and cut into foot-long strips until it is ¼ inches wide. Over half of these strips spoon a total of 5 to 6 tablespoons of filling at well-spaced intervals. Cover each strip with another strip of pasta. Seal by pressing down well on the borders. Cut each filled strip into ¼-inch tortelli, placing each on a lightly floured dishcloth as you go. (The action of cutting seals the pasta sides together.)

4 Boil the tortelli in plenty of boiling, salted water. Drain when cooked but still firm to the bite. Make sure that the pasta is well cooked in the thickest part.

5 Serve the tortelli with Parmesan cheese.

Over the years, this pasta-dough recipe has proved to be the most successful of all, with the semolina adding color, flavor and texture. You can use the dough to make pappardelle, tagliatelle, tortellini, ravioli, lasagne, etc. Cooking the potatoes in their skins means that the potato flesh will absorb much less water than it would if they were peeled. It also means that the starch remains in the flesh, rather than passing into the water, which allows the potato to retain more flavor. Leave the potatoes until cool enough to handle, then simply slide the skins off. Italian "00" flour is a very fine, white flour, available at some specialty foods shops.

SPAGHETTI ALLE OLIVE

Spaghetti with Olives

Such a wide variety of olives is available now that you can use your imagination and experiment with the type that you like the most. Choose green or black, and drain them well before using to get rid of as much brine as possible. You can marinate your own. The Gaeta olive, which comes from near Rome, is wonderful rinsed, dried, then left for 10 days in an infusion of extra virgin olive oil with fennel seeds, garlic and a little chile.

SERVES 4

⅔ cup good-quality olive oil

1 yellow bell pepper, cored, de-seeded and sliced

3 tomatoes, skinned and chopped

sea salt and freshly ground black pepper

3½ ounces olives, drained, halved and pitted

10 ounces spaghetti

2½ ounces pecorino or Parmesan, freshly grated

a handful of fresh flat-leaf parsley, finely chopped

1 Heat the oil in a heavy pan, and add the yellow pepper, tomato and salt and pepper to taste. Cover and simmer gently for 20 minutes, stirring occasionally. Add the olives and cook for 5 minutes.

2 Meanwhile cook the spaghetti in plenty of boiling, salted water until al dente. Drain thoroughly and add to the sauce.

3 Fold gently to mix, then pile into a warmed serving dish and sprinkle with the cheese and parsley. Serve at once.

Olives contain good quantities of vitamins A and E (although less of the latter than does the oil). Like the oil, they contain monounsaturated fatty acids, so they are protective of the heart and blood vessels and can help lower cholesterol levels. Olives that have been kept in brine contain a high level of sodium.

SPAGHETTI AGLIO OLIO E PEPERONCINO

Spaghetti with Garlic and Chile Oil

This is definitely a standby recipe, but it is simple and tasty. I often cook it when I've just come back from holiday and there's nothing else in the fridge.

SERVES 4

10 ounces spaghetti

4 tablespoons best-quality olive oil

2 garlic cloves, peeled

1 fresh hot red chile pepper (*peperoncino*), seeded and chopped

a handful of fresh flat-leaf parsley, finely chopped

freshly grated Parmesan to taste (optional)

1 Cook the spaghetti in plenty of boiling, salted water until al dente.

2 Meanwhile, heat the oil in a heavy sauté pan, add the whole garlic cloves and chile, and sauté gently until the garlic browns slightly.

3 Drain the spaghetti thoroughly and pile into a warmed serving dish.

4 Discard the garlic and chile. Add the parsley to the flavored oil, then mix well and pour over the spaghetti. Serve at once, with Parmesan if desired.

Garlic has many health-giving properties: it contains vitamins and many minerals, and sulphur compounds that are responsible for its flavor and odor. The smell of it cooking stimulates the production of gastric juices, so before you've even eaten it, it's started the process of good digestion.

LASAGNE CON MELANZANE
Lasagne with Eggplant

Lasagne have been enjoyed in Italy since Roman times. Baking pasta in layers with vegetables is healthy, tasty and very filling, and this is a perfect dish for sharing with family or friends.

SERVES 4

4 tablespoons good-quality olive oil

1 large garlic clove, peeled and crushed

1 large white onion, peeled and chopped

1¾ cups (14 ounces) chopped tomatoes

3 tablespoons red wine

sea salt and freshly ground black pepper

1 large firm, ripe eggplant

6 ounces egg lasagne (fresh pasta sheets, no pre-cooking required)

1 pound mozzarella cheese, sliced

a handful of fresh basil leaves

1 In a large saucepan heat half of the olive oil, then add the garlic and cook gently for a few minutes. Add the onion and sauté until soft. Lower the heat, add the tomatoes, wine, salt and pepper to taste, and simmer for 20 minutes. Set aside.

2 Cut the eggplant into lengthwise slices ⅛ inch thick, and place in layers in a colander, sprinkling salt between the layers. Set aside for 15 minutes. Rinse to remove the salt, and pat dry.

3 Meanwhile, preheat the oven to 400°.

4 In a frying pan, heat some of the remaining oil, just enough to cover the bottom. Sauté the eggplant slices quickly, about 2 minutes on each side, or until soft. Drain on paper towels. Continue in this fashion, using more oil as needed.

5 To assemble the lasagne, spread one-third of the tomato sauce in a baking dish (about 10 inches square). Add a layer of lasagne sheets and then a little more sauce, then half of the eggplant and mozzarella slices. Season the cheese with salt and pepper and sprinkle with some basil leaves. Continue in this way, finishing off with a layer of tomato sauce. Cover with foil.

6 Bake the lasagne in the preheated oven for 25 minutes or until bubbling.

This baked dish can be made a day ahead, so is particularly useful when entertaining. In Italy, eggplant are known as "poor man's meat" because they are so substantial and satisfying.

LASAGNE DI RADICCHIO ALLA TREVISANA

Radicchio Lasagne

I have a tremendous love for radicchio, having watched it being grown by my father. From planting to harvest is six weeks, so it would be a good vegetable to grow at home. There are two varieties: the Verona, which is round, and the Treviso, which is long and thin. Do try to get the Treviso – order it from your grocer – since it is very much less bitter and much more flavorful.

SERVES 4

3 heads Treviso radicchio

3 tablespoons olive oil

1 medium fennel bulb, peeled and quartered

11 ounces dried lasagne verdi (green pasta sheets)

1 onion, peeled and finely chopped

6 tablespoons butter

½ cup all-purpose flour

1 garlic clove, peeled and crushed

2 cups plus 2 tablespoons milk

sea salt and freshly ground black pepper

5½ ounces Dolcelatte (creamy blue) cheese, cut into cubes

1 Preheat the oven to 400°.

2 Quarter the radicchio, wash well and pat dry. Place on a baking sheet and drizzle with the oil. Bake for 10 minutes. The radicchio pieces will change color and become slightly charred; this is correct, because the flavor will be at its best. Set aside.

3 Meanwhile, steam the fennel pieces over boiling water, about 12 minutes (until slightly al dente). Remove and finely chop.

4 Cook the lasagne in plenty of boiling, salted water until al dente. Drain and set aside.

5 Now for the sauce. Cook the onion in a saucepan in the butter until it is softened and golden. Add the flour, garlic and steamed fennel and cook for a few minutes to remove the raw taste from the flour. Now add the milk, and some salt and pepper. Remove from the heat and stir vigorously with a wooden spoon.

6 Place the saucepan back on the heat and bring to a boil, stirring continuously until thickened. Add the cubed Dolcelatte and stir well. Add more salt and pepper if necessary.

7 To assemble the dish, place a layer of sauce in an oval ovenproof dish followed by a layer of radicchio and a layer of pasta, and continue in this fashion until all the sauce, radicchio and lasagne have been used up. Finish with sauce on top.

8 Place in the heated oven and bake for 20 minutes until golden.

A friend told me that soaking radicchio for half an hour removes much of its bitterness. However, it is this very bitterness that the Italians crave, believing that it is a stimulant of the liver, the cornerstone of health.

FARFALLE ALLA POLCERVERASCA

Pasta with Butter and Marjoram

This is a recipe I'd like to dedicate to tired cooks. If you've been working all day you want something tasty and simple, and the flavors here just seem to hit the right note. It's also very quick, just what you need when you're hungry. (If you want it to cook even more quickly, use a thinner pasta.)

SERVES 4

6 tablespoons unsalted butter
1 tablespoon (½ ounce) pine nuts, chopped
1 tablespoon chopped fresh marjoram
sea salt and freshly ground black pepper
10 ounces farfalle (bowtie-shaped pasta)
3 ounces Parmesan, freshly grated

1 Melt the butter in a small pan, add the pine nuts and marjoram and heat, stirring, for 1 minute. Season with salt and pepper.

2 Meanwhile, cook the farfalle in boiling, salted water until al dente. Drain, transfer to a heated serving bowl and mix well with the butter sauce.

3 Sprinkle with the Parmesan, and serve at once.

Marjoram is good for migraines, and for insomnia, so try to include it in a dish you eat at night. It is also a good antiseptic herb, guarding against infection, but not as strong as its sister, oregano.

VERMICELLI AL RANCETTO

Vermicelli in Tomato and Marjoram Sauce

This sauce is incredibly simple. If you grow your own herbs, it's wonderful to include some freshly picked marjoram in the tomato sauce, to give a pungent flavor. You could replace the marjoram with another herb, such as oregano or a soft-leaved thyme.

SERVES 4

4 tablespoons good-quality olive oil
1 onion, peeled and sliced
1 tablespoon chopped fresh marjoram
a handful of fresh flat-leaf parsley, finely chopped
8 ounces canned or fresh plum tomatoes, skinned
sea salt and freshly ground black pepper
10 ounces vermicelli (thin spaghetti)
2 ounces pecorino cheese, grated

1 Heat the oil in a medium saucepan. Add the onion and sauté until golden. Add the marjoram, parsley and tomatoes, and break the latter up with a wooden spoon. Season with salt and pepper, and simmer, covered, for 20 minutes.

2 Cook the vermicelli in boiling, salted water until al dente, then drain thoroughly and transfer to a heated serving dish.

3 Add the sauce and cheese to the hot pasta, mix well, and serve at once.

Marjoram is also known as a digestive herb, and its inclusion in a dish helps your body to assimilate the other constituents of the dish.

PENNE AL CAVOLFIORE

Penne with Cauliflower

This vegetable is most commonly served covered with a cheese sauce. Please think again, and use it with pasta as here, married with chile, a fantastic combination. Cauliflower is particularly associated with southern Italy, so don't expect to find it very often on menus in the north.

SERVES 4

- 1½ tablespoons olive oil
- 2 garlic cloves, peeled and chopped
- 1 small fresh, hot red chile pepper (*peperoncino*), whole or chopped
- 1 small cauliflower, cut into florets
- 7 ounces canned or fresh chopped tomatoes
- a handful of fresh flat-leaf parsley, chopped
- 4 fresh sage leaves, finely chopped
- sea salt and freshly ground black pepper
- 1 cup Vegetable Stock (page 61) or water
- 10 ounces penne (quill-shaped pasta)
- ¾ cup heavy cream

1 Heat the oil in a large pan and add the garlic and the chile pepper. Cook for 3 minutes over low heat, then add the cauliflower florets. After 5 minutes add the tomatoes in their juices, the herbs and salt and pepper, and cook gently for 10 minutes.

2 Add the stock; depending on the amount of cauliflower, you may need less stock, so do use your judgment.

3 Let simmer while you cook the pasta in plenty of boiling, salted water until al dente.

4 Add the cream to the cauliflower mixture. Remove the chile if whole, then coarsely mash the cauliflower with a potato masher.

5 Drain the pasta, transfer to a heated serving dish and stir in the sauce. Serve at once.

Cauliflower contains vitamins A, B and C, and the minerals potassium, iron and calcium. It's said to be good for arthritic and rheumatic conditions.

PENNETTE IN PADELLA

Penne in the Pan

Penne are tubes of pasta that resemble small quill pens. They are either ridged or smooth, and they can vary in length (pennette are slightly smaller than penne). This recipe was devised by the Lungarotti family, who own a charming hotel, vineyard and wine museum in Torgiano, Umbria, very near where I teach. They produce some excellent wine, their most famous one being San Giorgio. If you get an opportunity to taste this wine, you will not be disappointed.

SERVES 4

1 medium, firm and ripe
   eggplant
sea salt
4 tablespoons best-quality
   olive oil
3 tablespoons red wine
freshly ground black pepper
1 small onion, peeled and
   finely chopped
1 garlic clove, peeled and
   crushed

14 ounces canned or fresh
   chopped tomatoes
10 ounces pennette or
   penne (quill-shaped pasta)
2 tablespoons heavy cream
1 tablespoon finely chopped
   fresh oregano
1 tablespoon finely chopped
   fresh flat-leaf parsley
2 tablespoons freshly grated
   Parmesan

1 Cut the peeled eggplant into small cubes, sprinkle with salt, place in a bowl, cover with a small plate and weight down. Set aside for 15 minutes. Rinse the eggplant cubes well to remove the salt, and pat dry.

2 Heat the oil in a frying pan, add the eggplant and fry for 5 minutes until golden. Add the wine and simmer for 5 minutes, then season with salt and pepper.

3 Add the onion, garlic and tomatoes to the eggplant, bring to a boil, then reduce heat and simmer for 15 minutes (add a little water if necessary).

4 Cook the pasta in boiling, salted water until al dente, then drain.

5 Just before serving stir the cream, oregano and parsley into the sauce, and add more salt and pepper if necessary.

6 Transfer the pasta to the pot, toss with the sauce and heat through. Serve in a warm dish with the Parmesan sprinkled on top.

Many people believe that it isn't necessary these days to salt or "degorge" eggplants, but I think it's still vital. The eggplants are tenderer, have more flavor and do not absorb as much of the cooking oil.

RIGATONI CON BROCCOLETTI E GORGONZOLA

Pasta with Broccoli and Gorgonzola

The combination of the four main ingredients here is particularly tasty, satisfying and nutritionally rich. Do try to find Italian pine nuts (from *Pinus pinea*, the stone pine), since they are longer, thinner and creamier – and therefore tastier – than the Asian varieties. They are incredibly expensive, even in Italy, because acid rain in Europe has diminished the yield. Keep them in the fridge once the package is opened to prevent the oils from turning rancid.

SERVES 4

- 3 tablespoons (1½ ounces) pine nuts
- 3½ ounces broccoli florets
- 3½ ounces cauliflower florets
- 2 tablespoons olive oil
- 1 red onion, peeled and finely chopped
- 1 teaspoon chopped fresh thyme
- sea salt and freshly ground black pepper
- 10 ounces rigatoni (short, ribbed noodles)
- 3½ ounces Gorgonzola cheese, diced

1 Toast the pine nuts on a sheet of foil under the broiler, turning them frequently until they are golden.

2 Steam the broccoli and cauliflower for about 8 minutes, depending on size, or until just tender.

3 Meanwhile, heat the oil in a sauté pan, add the onion and cook until softened, then add the thyme and some salt and pepper.

4 Cook the pasta in plenty of boiling, salted water until al dente. Drain well and transfer to a heated serving dish.

5 Add the cheese to the onion along with the pine nuts, broccoli and cauliflower. Toss thoroughly into the pasta. Add more salt and pepper, if necessary, and serve.

All blue cheeses contain natural penicillin, which helps to boost the immune system. This particular sauce is very good for you (and tastes delicious).

BUCATINI ALLA SIRACUSANA

Syracusan-Style Pasta

To my mind there is no pasta dish that has more zing and personality than this one, from Syracuse in Sicily. It has all the right attributes of spiciness, flavor, color and drama, all very characteristic of Sicilian food and life, both in turn displaying many influences from North Africa and Greece.

SERVES 4

1 small eggplant

sea salt

2 tablespoons olive oil

2 garlic cloves, peeled and
   crushed

3 ripe plum tomatoes, chopped

1 small yellow bell pepper,
   de-seeded and cut into
   thin strips

10 black olives, pitted and
   chopped

10 capers, rinsed and drained

freshly ground black pepper

10 ounces bucatini
   (thick, hollow spaghetti),
   or any favorite pasta shape

a handful of fresh basil,
   roughly torn

freshly grated Pecorino
   Romano cheese to taste

1 Peel the eggplant, cut into cubes, then put in a colander, sprinkle with salt, weight down, cover and set aside to degorge moisture for 15 minutes. Rinse and pat dry.

2 In a large saucepan heat the olive oil and gently sauté the garlic until soft. Add the eggplant and cook until the cubes become soft and golden, about 8 minutes.

3 Add the tomatoes, yellow bell pepper, olives, capers and salt and pepper to taste. Mix well, cover the pan and cook for 20 minutes.

4 Cook the pasta in plenty of boiling, salted water until al dente. Drain and return to the pot. Add the sauce and basil, and mix well. Serve with the cheese sprinkled on top.

Never add fresh basil at the beginning of cooking, always at the end, because it is so tender and its volatile oils are destroyed by heat. These oils can also be lost on the chopping board, which is why I always tear or shred it.

ROTOLO RIPIENO

Spinach Pasta Roll

I've eaten this pasta roll only in the north of Italy. I'm using a classic spinach filling here, but you could also try a mushroom or ricotta filling. It makes an impressive dinner-party piece, particularly memorable because the grilling at the end makes the pasta become crisp.

SERVES 4 TO 6

Pasta

1½ cups Italian "00" (soft wheat) or cake (not self-rising) flour
1½ cups fine semolina flour
a pinch of sea salt
2 large eggs
1 tablespoon olive oil

Filling

4 tomatoes
12 ounces fresh spinach
¾ cup (6 ounces) ricotta cheese
freshly grated nutmeg
sea salt and freshly ground black pepper

To serve

2 tablespoons butter
1 ounce Parmesan, freshly grated

1 Make the pasta as for Potato Tortelli (pages 34–5). Cover with a dishcloth and set aside.

2 To make the filling, put the tomatoes in a bowl, cover with boiling water for about 30 seconds, then plunge into cold water, drain and skin. Chop the flesh.

3 Wash but do not dry the spinach and put in a saucepan with only the water still clinging to the leaves. Cook over low heat for 5 minutes, then drain well, squeezing out the excess water.

Finely chop the spinach and put in a bowl. Add the tomato, ricotta, nutmeg, salt and pepper and mix well together.

4 Roll out the pasta dough to a rectangular sheet about ⅛ inch thick. Spread the filling over the dough, leaving a ¼-inch border. Roll up the dough like a jelly roll, and then wrap in a piece of muslin, securing the ends with string.

5 Place the roll in a long, narrow, flameproof casserole or roasting pan, and cover

with lightly salted cold water. Bring to a boil and simmer for 20 minutes on the stove. Remove the roll from the water and leave to cool for 5 minutes.

6 Remove the muslin and cut the roll into ¾-inch-thick slices. Place slightly over-lapping in a buttered ovenproof dish. Melt the butter and drizzle over the slices. Sprinkle with the Parmesan and broil until lightly browned on top (ca. 7 minutes). Serve immediately.

Butter infused with sage leaves is excellent for drizzling over the top of the rotolo.

FETTUCCINE CON DUE FORMAGGI E PISTACCHI

Fettuccine with Two-Cheese Sauce and Pistachios

This pasta dish is blissfully simple and very colorful because of the green nuts and leaves. It's a pantry recipe, easy to put together at the end of the day. The fettuccine, being long and thin, is excellent with a rich cheese sauce.

SERVES 4

⅔ cup heavy cream

1½ ounces Dolcelatte or other creamy blue cheese

1½ ounces Parmesan, freshly grated

¼ cup (1 ounce) shelled pistachio nuts

sea salt and freshly ground black pepper

10 ounces fettuccine (ribbon noodles)

a handful of fresh basil, torn

1 Pour the cream into a saucepan and slowly bring to a boil. Reduce the heat, crumble in the Dolcelatte, and stir until melted and smooth. Add the Parmesan, and cook over very low heat until thick and smooth, a few minutes only.

2 Coarsely chop the pistachio nuts. Add to the sauce and season with salt and pepper to taste.

3 Cook the pasta in plenty of boiling, salted water until al dente. Drain, transfer to a heated serving dish, then stir in the sauce. Garnish with basil leaves and serve hot.

Pistachio nuts are related to the cashew nut and mango and, like all nuts, are high in vegetable protein. This protein, allied with the cheese and pasta, makes for a dish rich in nutrients.

FETTUCCINE E CECI
ALLA NAPOLETANA

Pasta with Chickpeas

This recipe is a good example of southern Italian cooking that does not rely heavily on meat, but provides carbohydrates and protein in the form of grain and legumes. The cheese provides extra nutrients.

SERVES 4

1 cup (7 ounces) dried
   chickpeas
4¼ cups water
3 bay leaves
3 tablespoons best-quality
   olive oil
5 tomatoes, skinned and
   chopped
1 garlic clove, peeled and
   crushed

a handful of fresh flat-leaf
   parsley, chopped
sea salt and freshly ground
   black pepper
10 ounces fettuccine
   (ribbon noodles)
a handful of fresh basil, torn
freshly grated Parmesan to
   taste (optional)

1 Soak the chickpeas overnight in plenty of cold water.

2 Drain chickpeas and place in a large pan with the 4¼ cups water and the bay leaves, boil for 10 minutes, then lower the heat and simmer for about 40 minutes or until tender.

3 Now add the oil, tomatoes, garlic and half the parsley to the chickpeas. Bring back to a boil, season with salt and pepper, then add the fettuccine. Cook for approximately 12 minutes, or until the pasta is tender. Add more water if required.

4 Add the remaining parsley and the basil and serve immediately, with Parmesan if desired.

Vegetables and legumes do not contain all the essential amino acids and so are known as incomplete proteins – except for soybeans, the only food of non-animal origin that is a complete protein. By combining a grain and a legume, as here, the nutritional value of the dish is considerably enhanced.

CANNELLONI CON VERDURE E FORMAGGIO

Cannelloni with Vegetables and Cheese

I have a great affinity for cannelloni, and in Italy we have many varieties. Many cannelloni dishes are made with pasta, but this one, traditional to Piacenza in Sicily, is constructed from crespelle, or pancakes, and is particularly light. It can be made into a wonderful antipasto dish.

SERVES 4

Crespella batter

2 cups all-purpose flour

½ teaspoon sea salt

1½ teaspoons freshly grated nutmeg

2 large eggs, beaten

1 large egg yolk, beaten

1½ cups whole milk

1 tablespoon unsalted butter, melted

3 tablespoons freshly grated Parmesan

freshly ground black pepper

Filling

1½ cups (12 ounces) ricotta cheese, well drained

1 large egg

⅔ cups (4½ ounces) broccoli, lightly cooked and chopped

3 tablespoons freshly grated Parmesan

4 ripe tomatoes, skinned, de-seeded and chopped

a handful of fresh flat-leaf parsley, chopped

1 teaspoon grated zest of unwaxed lemon

To cook and serve

3 tablespoons unsalted butter, melted

freshly grated Parmesan to taste

1 Preheat the oven to 400°.

2 To make the crespella batter, sift the flour, salt and nutmeg together into a large bowl. Add the eggs, egg yolk, milk and butter. Whisk the mixture until smooth. If it seems too thin, add a little more flour; if it is too thick, add a little milk. Beat in the Parmesan and some pepper.

3 To make the filling, in a large bowl combine the ricotta and the egg. Add the remaining filling ingredients and stir.

4 To cook the crespelle, lightly butter a 6- to 8-inch crêpe pan or a frying pan, and heat over medium heat. When hot, add a ladleful of the batter, and swirl the pan to make sure the pan is evenly coated with a thin layer of batter. Cook for 2 minutes or until lightly browned on the underside. Flip the crespella over and cook the other side until lightly browned. Remove the crespella and place on a paper towel, and repeat the process. Lightly grease the pan every so often to prevent the batter from sticking. You should make about 8 pancakes.

5 Spread about an eighth of the filling over each crespella and roll up into a cylinder. Place them in a single layer, seam side down, in a suitably sized, buttered ovenproof dish. Drizzle the melted butter over them and sprinkle generously with Parmesan.

6 Bake for 10 to 15 minutes in the preheated oven until piping hot and golden. Serve immediately.

This is a highly nutritious dish, the vegetables and cheese served in a pancake wrapping made with protein-rich eggs and whole milk. It can be made ahead of time; you can make the rolls smaller or larger; and you can use your creative talents with the filling.

54

RISOTTO

Pasta may rule in most of Italy but rice reigns in the north, and risotto is the preferred and most popular rice dish. You will find it everywhere, from Milan to Venice and from Turin to Como, on restaurant menus and on family dining tables. It is a healthy dish, since the nutrients of the grain are usually melded with those of vegetables, and then grated Parmesan cheese is added, contributing its protein and calcium.

Risotto is a dish that is simple to prepare, nutritious, economical, versatile and – as you will discover – addictively delicious. It is prepared with a short-grain, highly glutenous rice grown in the Po Valley of northern Italy. This comes in several different varieties, the most important of which are *Vialone Nano*, *Carnaroli* and *Arborio*. Vialone, which has a slightly shorter grain, is used mostly in fishy risottos, Carnaroli is normally allied with vegetables, and Arborio can be used in most dishes. Risotto rice is special in that it absorbs, to an unusual degree, the flavors of the ingredients with which it's cooked. It also merges with its cooking liquid to create a consistency that the Italians call

all'onda ("with waves"), while each individual grain of rice remains firm and al dente. This combination of full-flavored, still firm grains of rice, bound with a velvety base, is what gives risotto its unique quality and special character.

No matter what different *condimento* (flavoring or ingredient) is used, every risotto is created in basically the same way. A wide sauté pan with quite high sides should be used. The *riso* (rice) is first combined with a *soffritto* (a combination of fat and flavoring, usually butter and shallot) to coat it with fat. Simmering *brodo* (broth, which must be fresh and homemade) is then added gradually to the rice, allowing the rice to absorb one ladleful at a time. The rice is stirred continuously with a wooden spoon over moderate heat. When the grains are tender but still firm, a final dose of flavoring and seasoning is added (salt added at the beginning would toughen the rice). Then the rice is allowed to rest before being served on warm plates.

In Italy risotto, like pasta, is considered a *primo piatto*, the first course of a typical meal that might contain several courses, brought to the table at carefully paced intervals.

BRODO DI VERDURE
Vegetable Stock

This is a basic vegetable stock, to be used in the making of all risottos, but it can also be used as the base of a soup. Store it in the fridge for up to 3 days; it can also be frozen.

MAKES 4¼ CUPS

2 onions

12 whole cloves

1 garlic clove, peeled

6 carrots, scrubbed and trimmed

4 leeks, washed

2 celery stalks

3 tablespoons unsalted butter

1 tablespoon olive oil

4 bay leaves

2 sprigs fresh thyme

a handful of fresh flat-leaf
   parsley

1 Peel both onions, then stud one of them with the cloves. Chop the other onion, along with the garlic, carrots, leeks and celery. (Keep the garlic separate from the other vegetables.)

2 Melt the butter and oil together in a large, heavy saucepan. Add the garlic and sauté for 2 minutes. Add the chopped onion, carrot, leek, and celery and the whole studded onion, and cook for 5 to 7 minutes until softened, stirring continuously.

3 Add 12¾ cups water, the bay leaves, thyme and parsley, and bring to a boil. Cover, reduce the heat, and simmer for 1½ hours.

4 Remove from the heat and leave to cool for 1½ hours.

5 Return the pan to the heat and simmer for 15 minutes. Strain the stock through a sieve and return the liquid to the pan, discarding the vegetables. Boil rapidly until reduced by half.

6 Allow to cool completely before storing in the fridge.

I have not listed salt or pepper in the ingredients above, since everything depends on taste, and on the individual recipe in which you want to use the stock. And you must never add salt before the stock is reduced, because it would have the effect of concentrating the saltiness.

RISOTTO CON I FUNGHI

Wild Mushroom Risotto

This risotto is very popular during mushroom season: September and October, and then January and February. You can use a variety of interesting mushrooms, which we can find easily in specialty foods shops and supermarkets. Think of chestnut mushrooms, girolles, oyster mushrooms – and, of course, cèpes, the famous porcini of Italy.

SERVES 4

7 ounces edible wild mushrooms
½ cup unsalted butter
2 garlic cloves, peeled and crushed
6 shallots, peeled and finely chopped
freshly ground black pepper
1 sprig fresh rosemary, finely chopped
1½ cups Vialone Nano risotto rice

4¼ cups hot Vegetable Stock (page 61)
sea salt
½ cup white wine, preferably dry
a handful of fresh flat-leaf parsley, chopped
3 ounces Parmesan, freshly grated, plus extra for serving

1 Wipe the mushrooms thoroughly to remove any grit, and then slice them.

2 In a heavy medium saucepan, melt half the butter, then add the garlic and shallot and sauté until slightly translucent. Then add the mushrooms, pepper and rosemary.

3 Add the rice and stir to coat in the mixture. Add a ladleful of hot stock and stir continuously at a slow boil until it has been absorbed by the rice. Keep adding the stock in this way, a ladleful at a time, until the stock is used up, stirring continuously, about 18 to 20 minutes. Remove from heat.

4 Stir in some salt, and the wine, parsley, remaining butter and Parmesan. Add more salt and pepper if necessary.

5 Cover and let stand for 1 minute to allow the rice to rest. Serve on hot plates, with extra grated Parmesan if desired.

The secret of a good risotto is not to stop stirring, which helps to develop the starch and make the risotto authentically and deliciously creamy. Warm plates are important too, because otherwise the hot rice would adhere to the cold plate, ruining its consistency, which must remain "wavy": all'onda.

RISOTTO ALLA MILANESE

Classic Saffron Risotto

Milan is the home of risotto, and although this particular risotto is very simple, it is probably the most often enjoyed, many households making it at least once a week. The smell of saffron is haunting and the risotto is very comforting.

SERVES 4

⅔ cup unsalted butter

1 tablespoon olive oil

6 shallots, peeled and finely chopped

freshly ground black pepper

7 tablespoons dry white wine

4¼ cups hot Vegetable Stock (page 61)

1½ cups risotto rice (Vialone Nano is the best here)

¼ teaspoon powdered or crumbled saffron

sea salt

3½ ounces Parmesan, freshly grated, plus extra for serving

4 tablespoons light cream

a handful of fresh flat-leaf parsley, finely chopped

1 Melt the butter with the oil in a medium heavy saucepan, add the shallot and some pepper, and sauté for 5 minutes until softened.

2 Add the wine and 7 tablespoons of the stock, and boil until reduced by half. Meanwhile keep the remaining stock just below simmering point in a separate saucepan.

3 Add the rice to the shallot and reduced liquid, and cook for 5 minutes, stirring continuously over medium heat. Add the saffron and a ladleful of the hot stock, and stir continuously until it has been absorbed by the rice. Keep adding stock in this way, a ladleful at a time, stirring continuously between each addition, until the rice is tender but firm, and the stock is used up, about 18 to 20 minutes.

4 Remove from the heat and stir in some salt, and the Parmesan, cream and parsley.

5 Cover and let stand for 1 minute to allow the rice to rest. Serve on hot plates, with extra grated Parmesan if desired.

Because saffron, the stamen of a crocus, is hand picked, it tends to be very expensive. Never be tempted to use more than a recipe states, because saffron is very strong. Spanish saffron is the best, but beware of imitations.

RISOTTO ALLA ZUCCA

Pumpkin Risotto

Pumpkin is eaten year-round in Italy, not just during the season. Fresh pumpkins are put in straw in cellars to preserve them; the flesh is bottled in olive oil and eaten as an antipasto. It is also used in pasta sauces, in tortelli, and in baked vegetable dishes.

SERVES 4

- 2 tablespoons unsalted butter
- 2 teaspoons olive oil
- 2 garlic cloves, peeled and crushed
- 6 shallots, peeled and finely chopped
- 1 (18-ounce) pumpkin, peeled, de-seeded and chopped
- 1½ cups Carnaroli risotto rice
- 4¼ cups hot Vegetable Stock (page 61)
- sea salt and freshly ground black pepper
- a handful of fresh flat-leaf parsley, chopped
- 4 tablespoons freshly grated Parmesan

1 In a heavy medium saucepan, melt the butter with the oil, then add the garlic and sauté until browned. Add the shallot and pumpkin, and cook gently until the pumpkin softens.

2 Add the rice and stir to coat in the pumpkin mixture. Add a ladleful of hot stock and stir continuously over moderate heat until it has been absorbed by the rice. Keep adding stock in this way until it is all used up and the rice is creamy and al dente, about 18 to 20 minutes. The rice should be al dente. Remove from heat.

3 Stir in some salt and pepper, the parsley and Parmesan.

4 Cover and let stand for 1 minute to allow the rice to rest, then serve at once on warmed plates.

Pumpkin flesh contains many vitamins and minerals. The yellow flesh is packed with beta-carotene, the precursor of vitamin A, so pumpkin is particularly good for the skin and the mucous membranes of the body. The seeds, which should always be saved for eating, are said to have a calming effect on the nervous system.

RISOTTO CON ZUCCHINI
E FIORI

Risotto with Zucchini and Their Flowers

This is a slightly indulgent recipe, since zucchini flowers are not readily available unless you grow them yourself. I have seen them in shops – at a price – but they always look rather tired, although they can be revived in iced water. Give them a shake before use to dislodge any insects that might be lurking inside. Whenever I see *fiori di zucchini*, it means the onset of summer for me.

SERVES 4

5 tablespoons olive oil

8 young, tender and thin
zucchini, sliced, whole
flowers detached

6 shallots, peeled and sliced

1½ cups Carnaroli risotto rice

freshly ground black pepper

4¼ cups hot Vegetable Stock
(page 61)

sea salt

a handful of fresh mint, finely
chopped

a handful of fresh flat-leaf
parsley, finely chopped

2 tablespoons unsalted butter

2 ounces Parmesan, freshly
grated, plus extra for serving

1 In a deep frying pan heat the oil, and fry the sliced zucchini for 2 minutes until tender.

2 Add the shallot and the rice, stir until coated in oil, then season with black pepper. Begin to add the hot stock, a ladleful at a time, stirring continuously over moderate heat. Wait for the rice to absorb each ladleful before adding any more. Continue until all the stock has been used up and the rice is creamy and al dente, about 18 to 20 minutes. Remove from heat.

3 Stir in the whole zucchini flowers, season with some salt, and stir in the mint, parsley, butter and Parmesan.

4 Cover and let stand for 1 minute to allow the rice to rest, then serve at once on warm plates, with extra Parmesan sprinkled on top, if desired.

The risotto tastes just as good simply made with young zucchini without the flowers.

RISOTTO ALLA PARMIGIANA

Parmesan Risotto

This is a good family recipe and one that children love; at least, my nieces and nephews do. It is rich, creamy and flavorsome without being too overpowering.

SERVES 4

½ cup unsalted butter

1 tablespoon olive oil

6 shallots, peeled and finely chopped

freshly ground black pepper

1½ cups Carnaroli risotto rice

4½ cups hot Vegetable Stock (page 61)

3 to 4 tablespoons dry white wine

sea salt

5½ ounces Parmesan, freshly grated

1 Melt the butter with the oil in a medium saucepan, add the shallots and some pepper, and sauté for 5 minutes until softened.

2 Add the rice and stir to coat in oil and butter. Now add a ladleful of hot stock, stirring continuously over moderate heat until it has been absorbed by the rice. Keep adding stock in this way until the rice is creamy and tender but firm and the stock is used up, about 18 to 20 minutes.

3 Stir in the wine, some salt and pepper and the Parmesan. Remove from heat.

4 Cover and let stand for 1 minute to let the rice rest, then serve at once on warmed plates.

Parmigiano Reggiano, the best Parmesan, is the king of Italian cheeses. There are very few cases of osteoporosis in Italy, because Parmesan, with its wealth of bone-nourishing calcium, is eaten in large quantities in every household.

RISOTTO AL RADICCHIO

Radicchio Risotto

Most people think of radicchio as bitter, but cooking it in this way makes it become sweeter. It's also very colorful. This recipe came from Madalena Chapello, a family friend; I spent an entire weekend with her, learning how to cook radicchio.

SERVES 4

6 tablespoons unsalted butter

1 tablespoon olive oil

6 shallots, peeled and finely chopped

1½ cups Carnaroli risotto rice

½ cup red wine

14 ounces Treviso radicchio, shredded

freshly ground black pepper

4¼ cups hot Vegetable Stock (page 61)

sea salt

3 ounces Parmesan, freshly grated, plus extra for serving

a handful of fresh basil, freshly torn

2 tablespoons finely chopped fresh flat-leaf parsley

1 In a medium saucepan melt half the butter with all the oil, then add the shallot and sauté until it becomes slightly translucent. Add the rice and mix well so that the rice is glistening.

2 Stir in the wine and shredded radicchio, and season with pepper. Add a ladleful of hot stock and stir continuously over moderate heat until it has been absorbed by the rice. Continue in this way, adding a ladleful of stock at a time and stirring continuously, until all the stock is used up, about 18 to 20 minutes. Remove from heat.

3 Season with some salt, and add the remaining butter and the Parmesan, basil and parsley. Add more salt and pepper if necessary.

4 Cover and let stand for 1 minute to allow the rice to rest. Serve at once on hot plates, with extra grated Parmesan if desired.

Radicchio, being a member of the chicory family of vegetables, is easy to digest when it has been cooked. It is available year-round, but it tends to have more strength of flavor in the winter.

SUPPLÍ DI RISO

Fried Risotto with Shallots, Orange Zest and Mozzarella

This recipe is not for a risotto, but for risotto rice that is cooked in almost exactly the same way, before being flavored, then formed into little balls and fried. In the south of Italy, we call them *arancini*, or "little oranges." We always seem to eat them when traveling on the boat to Sicily.

SERVES 4

- ¼ cup unsalted butter
- 1¼ cups Arborio risotto rice
- 3⅔ cups hot Vegetable Stock (page 61)
- 6 ounces mozzarella cheese, grated or diced
- 6 shallots, peeled and finely chopped
- a handful of mixed fresh herbs, chopped
- zest of 1 large unwaxed orange, grated
- 6 tablespoons freshly grated Parmesan
- sea salt and freshly ground black pepper
- 1 egg
- 1 cup fresh breadcrumbs
- 6 tablespoons olive oil

1 Melt the butter in a large saucepan, stir in the rice and brown for a few minutes. Stir in a ladleful of hot stock and cook, stirring continuously, until the liquid has been absorbed. Continue doing this until the rice is cooked and all the stock is used up, about 20 minutes. Remove from heat.

2 Now add the cheese, shallot, herbs, orange zest, Parmesan, and some salt and pepper. Stir to combine, and leave to cool.

3 Form the flavored rice into balls the size of a plum. Beat the egg and roll the rice balls first in the egg and then in the breadcrumbs until covered.

4 Heat the oil in a frying pan and fry the rice balls until golden on all sides. Drain on paper towels and serve hot or cold.

There are many possible combinations and fillings for supplí. *For example, the flavored rice given here could be wrapped around a cube of cheese or a bit of meat.*

RISOTTO DI SPINACI

Spinach Risotto

This is dedicated to real spinach lovers like me. In Italy spinach appears on the menu at all times of the year, since Italians believe that, eaten daily, it is the key to good health. We have many ways of enjoying it, as a result, and this recipe is one.

SERVES 4

2¼ pounds spinach leaves

6 tablespoons unsalted butter

6 shallots, peeled and finely
   chopped

1½ cups Arborio risotto rice

⅛ cup white wine

freshly ground black pepper

4¼ cups hot Vegetable Stock
   (page 61)

freshly grated nutmeg

sea salt

3 ounces Parmesan, freshly
   grated, plus extra for serving

1 Steam the spinach for a few minutes until soft. Drain very thoroughly, squeeze dry and chop finely.

2 In a medium saucepan melt half the butter and sauté the shallot until softened. Add the rice and cook, stirring, over moderate heat for a few minutes, then add the spinach, the wine and some black pepper and stir to combine.

3 Add a ladleful of hot stock, and stir continuously until this has been absorbed by the rice.

Continue to add stock in this manner, a ladleful at a time, stirring continuously, until it is used up and the rice is creamy, about 18 to 20 minutes. Remove from heat.

4 Stir in the nutmeg, the remaining butter, some salt and the Parmesan.

5 Cover and let stand for 1 minute to allow the rice to rest. Serve at once on hot plates, and add extra Parmesan at the table if desired.

Spinach's iron and calcium are not readily available because of its oxalic acid content, so it is not as nutritious as we have been led to believe. However, being green, it contains vitamins A and C – and of course it tastes delicious!

RISI E BISI

Risotto with Peas

This recipe has become a specialty of Venice because of the wonderful soil of the Veneto, where peas grow in abundance. In the pea season, there is often such a glut that the vendors don't bother to weigh them out but just pour the pods freely into your bag, so that you can be sure to enjoy them at their very finest and sweetest.

SERVES 4

2¼ pounds sweet fresh
    pea pods, young and tender
¼ cup unsalted butter
2 tablespoons olive oil
6 shallots, peeled and finely
    sliced
2 garlic cloves, peeled and
    finely chopped
a handful of fresh flat-leaf
    parsley, chopped

4¼ cups hot Vegetable Stock
    (page 61)
1½ cups Vialone Nano
    risotto rice
½ cup dry white wine
freshly ground black pepper
sea salt
a handful of fresh mint, chopped
2 ounces Parmesan, freshly
    grated, plus extra for serving

1 Shell and rinse the peas. In a medium saucepan melt the butter with the oil and sauté the shallot and garlic until they become slightly translucent, then stir in the parsley, peas and just enough hot stock to barely cover the ingredients. Simmer gently for 2 minutes.

2 Add the rice, wine and some pepper, and stir to coat the rice with this mixture, using a wooden spoon. Add a ladleful of hot stock, and stir continuously over moderate heat until it has been absorbed by the rice. Continue to add stock in this manner, one ladleful at a time, stirring continuously until all the stock is used up and the rice is creamy, about 18 to 20 minutes. Remove from heat.

3 Stir in some salt, then the mint and Parmesan.

4 Cover and let stand for 1 minute to allow the rice to rest, then serve on warmed plates, with extra grated Parmesan if desired.

Because they are green, peas contain rich supplies of vitamins A and C. They are a stimulant and supply energy. They should be eaten as fresh as possible because, when plucked from the plant, their sugars rapidly convert to starch.

RISOTTO DI FINOCCHIO

Fennel Risotto

The Italians love to eat fennel, either raw or cooked. Fennel bulbs are male or female: the females are plump with hips, and the males are long and thin. Do choose both in your cooking, since cooked together they support each other as far as flavor is concerned.

SERVES 4 TO 6

1 pound 2 ounces fennel bulbs
6 tablespoons unsalted butter
6 shallots, peeled and finely
    chopped
1½ cups Arborio risotto rice
freshly ground black pepper
4¼ cups hot Vegetable Stock
    (page 61)

sea salt
zest of 2 unwaxed lemons,
    finely grated
a handful of fresh flat-leaf
    parsley, finely chopped
3 ounces Parmesan, freshly
    grated

1 Wash and trim the fennel, removing all the hard external green bits. Cut the fennel into thin, even slices.

2 In a medium saucepan melt half the butter and sauté the fennel and shallot for about 5 minutes until tender. Add the rice and stir until it is glistening with butter.

3 Season with pepper, then gradually add the hot stock, a ladleful at a time, stirring continuously over moderate heat and allowing the rice to absorb the liquid before adding more.

Keep stirring and adding stock, ladleful by ladleful, until it is used up and the rice is creamy, about 18 to 20 minutes. Remove from heat.

4 Stir in some salt, the lemon zest, parsley, the remaining butter and the Parmesan.

5 Cover and allow the rice to rest for 1 minute, then stir once more before serving on warmed plates. Eat at once.

Fennel often appears on the table at the end of a meal in Italy, to be eaten raw as a digestive. The male fennel is best for this, since it is less fibrous. The alkalinity of fennel aids digestion, helping to metabolize the fat in a rich meal.

FAGIOLI

Dried peas, beans and lentils are known collectively as legumes. Because they are seeds, they are very nutritious, containing everything needed for the next generation of plants, just as grains do. All legumes are rich in incomplete protein, so the most nutritious way of eating them is with grains, whose amino acids will help to balance those of the legume. Legumes contain no cholesterol and very little fat, and they are good sources of B vitamins, calcium, iron, potassium, magnesium and zinc.

The fresh peas, beans and lentils that become the familiar dried legumes are harvested in late summer. I love to see fresh beans in Italian markets, their speckled and shiny pods bursting with ripe seeds. They are more common in their dried form in Italy, and they are enjoyed there throughout the winter months as a source of nutrients when fresh vegetables are less available.

In Italy we have a vast array of legumes: borlotti (pinto) and cannellini beans, *lenticchie* (lentils), fava (broad) beans, *ceci* (chickpeas) and *piselli* (peas), to name but a few. We enjoy them particularly in the south of Italy. I was brought up on a varied diet of legumes, mainly due to the fact that southern Italians concentrate on growing vegetables and other crops rather than on rearing animals such as cattle. (Beef and butter, for instance, are much more northern in culinary terms.) My grandmother had a huge collection of legume recipes that I learned from her and am happy to share with you.

There are some golden rules you must follow in the cooking of legumes, but otherwise they are blissfully straightforward, quick and easy to prepare. First of all, buy your supplies from a market with a fast turnover, so that you can be sure they are not too old. All legumes – apart from lentils – must be soaked in lots of cold water, at least overnight, in order to rehydrate them. They should then be covered with fresh, cold water, brought to a boil and cooked for 10 minutes; this is in order to inactivate potentially toxic substances many legumes contain. Thereafter, continue cooking the legumes – perhaps with some added flavoring, such as a couple of bay leaves and/or a sprig of fresh thyme – for another 40 minutes, at a slow simmer, or until they are tender. Lentils do not require soaking, and they will only need simmering for about 30 minutes. Salt legumes only after cooking; doing so before will toughen the skins.

A handy rule of thumb is that legumes, when cooked, roughly double in volume and weight: so 8 ounces dried beans will become roughly 16 ounces after cooking. And don't be ashamed to use canned beans if you haven't got time to soak dried beans; simply drain and rinse them, and heat through for a few minutes before using in a recipe.

ZUPPA DELLA NONNA CON LENTICCHIE E PATATE

Grandmother's Lentil and Potato Soup

This soup brings back a rush of family and childhood memories. It smells so enticing, and its texture is wonderful. The Italians traditionally eat lentils at the New Year because they represent money, and therefore potential success in the coming year. The best to use are the *lenticchie di Norcia*, tiny green lentils that are very expensive because they are hand picked. They are also considered holy, because they grow in the sacred land near Assisi.

SERVES 4

10 new potatoes, preferably Italian, scrubbed

sea salt

1 cup (8 ounces) small dried green lentils

3 tablespoons olive oil

20 ounces tomato passata (strained tomatoes) or chopped tomatoes

freshly ground black pepper

2 garlic cloves, peeled and crushed

2 ounces Parmesan, freshly grated

a handful of fresh flat-leaf parsley, chopped

1 Cut the potatoes into even-sized cubes without removing the skins. Put into a medium saucepan and add 3¾ cups boiling water. Season with salt and boil for 10 minutes.

2 Add the lentils, oil, tomato, pepper and crushed garlic. Bring to a boil, then cover and simmer for 40 minutes. Check and adjust the seasoning.

3 Serve sprinkled with the Parmesan and parsley.

Lentils are 50 percent carbohydrate and 25 percent protein; they also contain a good quantity of iron and fiber. If you have the rind of a piece of Parmesan lurking in your fridge, do use it in this soup (or any other soup), to enrich the flavor. Whoever is served the rind should make a wish! And to make a dried-out piece of Parmesan assume some of its former glory, wrap it overnight in a damp dishcloth.

MINESTRA DI CECI E PEPERONI

Chickpea and Pepper Soup

This is a family soup that is often served in our village, since we produce so many peppers and chickpeas. It's colorful, full of flavor and very satisfying.

SERVES 4

1¼ cups (9 ounces) dried chickpeas

2 red onions, peeled and chopped

2 tablespoons fruity olive oil

2 potatoes, peeled and diced

3 red bell peppers, de-seeded and cut into strips

1 carrot, peeled and finely chopped

3 ripe tomatoes, cut into chunks

2 garlic cloves, peeled and crushed

sea salt and freshly ground black pepper

a handful of fresh flat-leaf parsley, finely chopped

extra virgin olive oil

1 Soak and cook the chickpeas as suggested on page 79. While the chickpeas are cooking, sauté the onion in the oil until softened, then add the potato, pepper, carrot, tomato, garlic and 4 tablespoons of water.

2 Bring to a boil, then cook for 15 minutes over moderate heat, stirring constantly to keep the vegetables from sticking (add a little more water if necessary). Season with salt and pepper.

3 The moment the chickpeas are cooked, pour the prepared sauce into them, stirring gently.

4 Serve the soup in bowls and sprinkle with parsley and olive oil. You may want to offer some grated Parmesan to sprinkle on top.

Peppers are high in nutrients such as vitamins A, B, C, and E and K. Red peppers contain more vitamin A – as beta-carotene – than the green. Many people believe that chickpeas have a diuretic effect, and that they can energize, preventing tiredness.

MINESTRA DI CECI E CASTAGNE

Chestnut Soup with Chickpeas

My father really loves this recipe, because he grows chestnuts in Avellino, in Campania. In Minori, my village, we have a torchlight festival at the end of October to celebrate the chestnut harvest. This soup is one of many ways in which we use chestnuts locally.

SERVES 4

1 cup (7 ounces) dried chickpeas
1 pound fresh chestnuts
3 celery stalks
4 bay leaves
7 tablespoons olive oil

4 garlic cloves, peeled
sea salt and freshly ground
    black pepper
4 slices country-style bread

1 Soak the chickpeas in water overnight.

2 Preheat the oven to 400°.

3 Score the chestnut skins on the outside – cutting into the skin slightly – and put on a baking sheet. Cook in the oven for 40 minutes.

4 Meanwhile, drain the soaked chickpeas, and put them in a large saucepan with 10½ cups fresh water. Add the celery, bay leaves and 2 tablespoons of the oil. Boil vigorously for 10 minutes. Lower the heat and simmer for 40 minutes until the chickpeas are tender and the cooking liquid has reduced.

5 When the chestnuts are done, remove from the oven and let cool slightly. Peel off the thick outer skin, then the inner skin. Heat the remaining oil in a frying pan and fry the peeled chestnuts and garlic until golden.

6 Remove the bay leaves and celery from the chickpea soup and stir in the chestnuts, garlic and oil from the pan. Season with salt and pepper.

7 Toast the bread slices. Put the slices in the bottom of a soup tureen and pour the soup over them. Let stand for 2 to 3 minutes before serving.

Chestnuts have high levels of carbohydrate, and very little fat. They are normally organic, since the trees are typically left to grow entirely naturally. Chestnuts can be used as a vegetable, a meat substitute, a flour for pasta or pastry, and in puddings.

JOTA

Bean and Cabbage Soup

This northern dish is eaten for *pranzo*, lunch, with a hunk of bread during the winter months. It's almost mandatory for all Italians to eat lots of beans during the winter, since they believe them to be synonymous with health, warmth and energy. Make this soup the day before to allow all the flavors to amalgamate.

SERVES 4

¾ cup (6 ounces) dried
   cannellini beans
1 medium fennel bulb,
   chopped
1 onion, peeled and chopped
2 garlic cloves, peeled and
   crushed

1 green cabbage, shredded
4 tablespoons tomato sauce
sea salt and freshly ground
   black pepper
2 tablespoons olive oil
a handful of fresh flat-leaf
   parsley, finely chopped

1 Soak and cook the cannellini beans as suggested on page 79.

2 When the beans have nearly finished their cooking (ca. 30 minutes), stir in the fennel, onion, garlic, cabbage, tomato sauce, salt and pepper, and simmer for 30 minutes or until the beans are tender.

3 Stir in the oil and parsley, check and add more salt and pepper if necessary, and serve.

Cabbage contains vitamins A, B and C; the darker the color of the leaves, the higher the content of nutrients.

PAPAZOI

Barley and Bean Soup

Here is a Roman soup that I tasted during a long, leisurely Sunday lunch at a local restaurant. It was the star of the show, and it took a long quizzing of the chef to persuade him to part with the recipe.

SERVES 6

1 cup (8 ounces) dried borlotti (pinto) beans
1 cup (7 ounces) Scotch barley
2 tablespoons olive oil
2 garlic cloves, peeled and crushed
8½ cups water or Vegetable Stock (page 61)
7 ounces potatoes, peeled and diced

½ cup fresh sweet corn kernels, scraped from the raw cob
a small handful fresh sage leaves, finely chopped
a handful of fresh flat-leaf parsley, finely chopped
sea salt and freshly ground black pepper

1 Soak the beans and barley, in separate bowls, overnight.

2 Heat the oil in a large saucepan, and add the garlic and the drained beans and barley. Pour in the water or stock, bring to a boil, and cook over a high heat for 10 minutes.

3 Lower the heat, add the potatoes, corn and sage, and cook more gently for 40 minutes.

4 Stir in the parsley, and season with salt and pepper. Serve immediately.

Scotch barley is healthier than pearl, since the husk has not been removed. Scotch also has a nuttier flavor, and normally needs to be cooked longer than pearl to soften and release the starches. These are what create the almost viscous texture of cooked barley, not too different from that of cooked risotto rice.

CIANFOTTA

Italian Bean Hot Pot

This warming and colorful stew is synonymous with Tuscany, where the food tends to be of a rich and substantial nature. You can try different combinations of vegetables to create your own hot pot. This is one of my favorites.

SERVES 4

1 cup plus 2 tablespoons
  (9 ounces) dried cannellini
  beans
1 small eggplant, diced
sea salt
4 tablespoons olive oil
1 onion, peeled and chopped
2 garlic cloves, peeled
2 celery stalks, chopped
1 teaspoon finely chopped
  fresh rosemary

2 yellow bell peppers,
  de-seeded and diced
2 potatoes, peeled and diced
1 pound fresh tomatoes, diced
½ teaspoon dried red pepper
  flakes
freshly ground black pepper
a handful of fresh flat-leaf
  parsley, chopped
a handful of fresh basil, torn

1 Soak and cook the cannellini beans as suggested on page 79.

2 While the beans are cooking, put the eggplant cubes into a colander, sprinkle with salt, cover and weight down, and leave for 15 to 20 minutes. Rinse the salt off and pat the cubes dry.

3 Heat the olive oil in a medium saucepan, add the onion and sauté until translucent, then add the garlic, celery and rosemary. Let these sauté for a few minutes as well, then add the remaining vegetables and the red pepper.

4 Stir well, cover lightly, and cook over low heat for 30 minutes. Add the cooked beans and cook for an additional 10 minutes.

5 Stir again, remove from heat and add the parsley and basil. Check and adjust the seasoning, and serve warm.

This could be called the Italian version of ratatouille, but because of the beans and potatoes – double carbohydrate – it's definitely a dish for the bitingly cold Tuscan winters.

MINESTRONE CON RISO E FAGIOLI

Vegetable Soup with Rice and Beans

In Italy there are a multitude of vegetable soups, or *minestrone:* roughly translated, the word means "mixture" or "hotchpotch." Countless ways exist for mixing good wholesome ingredients in a soup – one for every day of the year – and this is a particular favorite of mine.

SERVES 4

2 garlic cloves, peeled and chopped

1 celery stalk, finely chopped

1 red onion, peeled and sliced

2 tablespoons olive oil

8 ripe, fresh, red tomatoes, skinned and chopped

2¼ cups (18 ounces) cooked borlotti (pinto) beans (see page 79)

1 cup (8 ounces) Arborio risotto rice

½ teaspoon dried red pepper flakes

a handful of fresh flat-leaf parsley, chopped

a handful of fresh mint, chopped

sea salt and freshly ground black pepper

extra virgin olive oil

1 In a large sauté pan, sauté the garlic, celery and onion in the oil until softened. Add the tomatoes and simmer for 10 minutes.

2 Put the cooked beans into a medium saucepan. Pour the sauce over the cooked beans, then add the rice and 3 cups water, stirring well.

3 Stir in the red pepper flakes, parsley and mint, and simmer for 20 minutes, until the rice is tender. You will need to add more water if the soup is looking too thick.

4 Season with salt and pepper, and serve with a drizzle of the oil.

This is a wonderful example of a complete protein, the marriage of legume and grain – beans and rice. It's a dish typical of the north, where people need fuel and energy for the colder weather.

MILLECOSEDDE
Thick Legume Soup

The texture of this soup is thick and lumpy. I ate enormous quantities of it when I was a student, since it is satisfying, hearty and very economical (just right when your budget is low). The food of Italy is so regional that soups similar to *millecosedde* are served from the top to the toe of the country, in thousands of different variations – roughly the meaning of its name.

SERVES 6

7 tablespoons olive oil

1 carrot, peeled and chopped

1 onion, peeled and chopped

1 garlic clove, peeled and finely chopped

8½ cups Vegetable Stock (page 61)

½ small cabbage, blanched and shredded

1 cup (8 ounces) cooked *borlotti* (pinto) beans (see page 79)

1 cup (8 ounces) cooked cannellini beans

1 cup (8 ounces) cooked chickpeas

½ cup (4 ounces) cooked green lentils

8 ounces mushrooms, finely sliced

sea salt and freshly ground black pepper

8 ounces farfalle (bowtie-shaped pasta) or other small pasta shapes

4 ounces Pecorino cheese, freshly grated

a handful of fresh flat-leaf parsley, finely chopped

1 Heat the oil in a large heavy pan, add the carrot, onion and garlic, and sauté gently for 5 minutes.

2 Add the stock and bring to a boil, then lower the heat, add the cabbage and simmer for 5 minutes.

3 Add the drained legumes and the mushrooms to the pan, and season with salt and pepper.

4 Stir well, add the pasta, and cook for an additional 10 minutes.

5 Sprinkle with cheese and parsley to serve.

INSALATA DI FAGIOLI DELLA NONNA

Grandmother's Bean Salad

Because Italian bread goes stale so quickly, we have an infinite number of recipes for using it up. This is a typical southern recipe with the hint of piquant heat that is so prevalent in the south.

SERVES 4

½ cup (4 ounces) dried
   cannellini beans
zest of 1 unwaxed lemon
6 tablespoons extra virgin
   olive oil
2 tablespoons red wine
   vinegar

½ teaspoon dried red pepper
   flakes
a handful of mixed fresh herbs
   (parsley, thyme and oregano)
3½ ounces country bread,
   cut into small cubes
sea salt and freshly ground
   black pepper

1 Soak and cook the cannellini beans as suggested on page 79. Drain the beans, and let them cool. Put the beans in a serving bowl.

2 In a separate bowl, combine the remaining ingredients, except for the bread and salt and pepper, and stir into the cooled beans.

3 Add the bread, toss, and season with salt and pepper. Serve immediately.

The combination of grain (bread) and legume enables the dish to be a complete source of protein.

PURE DI FAVE CON CICORIA

Chicory with Mashed Cannellini Beans

In Italy there are several types of chicory: escarole, prickly-leafed chicory, frizzy *frisée*, blanched Belgian endive and the radicchios all belong to the chicory family. They are bitter in flavor, and they marry well with the comparative sweetness of the beans. You may like to cook the chicory first: blanch it only, so that it remains al dente, or brush with olive oil and grill as with radicchio.

SERVES 4

1 cup (8 ounces) cooked
    cannellini beans (see page 79)
1 garlic clove, peeled and
    pressed
2 tablespoons extra virgin
    olive oil
2 teaspoons fresh marjoram,
    chopped
1 tablespoon lemon juice

zest of 1 unwaxed lemon,
    grated
sea salt and freshly ground
    black pepper
2 heads chicory or escarole
1 ounce black olives, pitted
a small handful of fresh flat-leaf
    parsley, chopped

1 Heat the cooked cannellini beans gently in a medium saucepan.

2 Mash the beans with a potato masher, together with the garlic. Then stir in the oil, marjoram, lemon juice and zest. Season with salt and pepper to taste.

3 Wash and dry the chicory leaves. Divide them between four plates and arrange the warm mashed beans on the leaves. Serve garnished with the olives and parsley.

A good balance of flavors, the bitter and the sweet, and a good balance of nutrients too. I like to keep a bean purée in the fridge for snacking and nibbling purposes. (They improve with age, but they don't keep longer than two days.)

INSALATA DEL CONTADINO

Farmer's Salad

Once, when I was walking in the fields surrounding the cooking school, I asked a couple of the workers what they were having for lunch, and it turned out to be this salad. Broccoli is grown locally in Umbria, although it is generally regarded as a southern Italian vegetable, appearing in the cooler months of the year.

SERVES 4

4 tablespoons extra virgin
    olive oil
3 tablespoons lemon juice
½ teaspoon dried red pepper
    flakes
sea salt and freshly ground
    black pepper

18 ounces broccoli florets
1 cup (8 ounces) cooked borlotti
    beans (see page 79)
a handful of fresh flat-leaf
    parsley, finely chopped

1 Make the dressing first. In a serving dish large enough to hold the beans and broccoli, combine the oil, lemon juice, red pepper flakes, and salt and pepper to taste.

2 Place the broccoli in a large pan of boiling salted water, and cook until al dente. Drain and add the broccoli to the dish with the dressing.

3 Add the cooked beans and parsley and mix well. Serve at room temperature.

A vitamin-C-enriched salad. Adding a little olive oil to the cooking water when boiling green vegetables helps them to retain their color.

TORTINO

Layered Zucchini and Barley Casserole

This barley dish makes a nutritious and wholesome meal served with crusty bread, followed by a crisp green salad. I hope this will become part of your weekly repertoire: it's real comfort food, eaten like a risotto. An ancient grain known as *farro* is also grown in Italy and is used in similar ways.

SERVES 4

1 cup (8 ounces) pearl barley

4¼ cups Vegetable Stock (page 61)

3 tablespoons olive oil

¼ cup butter

1 pound zucchini, sliced

2 garlic cloves, peeled and crushed

6 ripe tomatoes, chopped

5½ ounces mozzarella cheese, diced

a handful of fresh basil, torn

a handful of fresh mint, chopped

a handful of fresh flat-leaf parsley, chopped

3½ ounces Parmesan, freshly grated

sea salt and freshly ground black pepper

1 cup fresh white bread-crumbs

1 In a large saucepan, cook the barley in the stock for 25 minutes, or until most of the stock has been absorbed.

2 Preheat the oven to 400°.

3 Heat the oil and butter in a frying pan, add the zucchini and garlic, and fry until golden. Drain the zucchini on paper towels and set aside.

4 Add the tomato and mozzarella to the barley with the basil, mint, parsley, Parmesan and salt and pepper to taste.

5 To assemble, arrange half the zucchini in a shallow ovenproof casserole dish in a single layer. Spread all of the barley mixture over the zucchini, and then add a final layer of the remaining zucchini.

6 Spread the breadcrumbs over, then bake for 20 minutes, or until golden brown.

Italians make a drink with barley – called bimbo *– that has energy-giving properties and is good for children and infants because it is easy to digest. In Britain as well, barley water is considered to be nutritive.*

FAGIOLINI E PATATE CON PESTO

Beans with Potatoes and Pesto

Try this wonderful way of enjoying pesto, rather than on pasta, which seems to be the most common usage. These three ingredients together produce something rather memorable.

SERVES 4

Pesto

3 garlic cloves, peeled

3 ounces fresh basil leaves

4 tablespoons extra virgin olive oil

3 tablespoons freshly grated Parmesan

1 tablespoon freshly grated Pecorino Romano cheese

2 tablespoons (1 ounce) pine nuts

To serve

9 ounces Italian new potatoes, scrubbed and quartered (Spunto is a good variety)

1 cup (8 ounces) cooked and drained cannellini beans (see page 79)

sea salt and freshly ground black pepper

1 Start by making the pesto. (I firmly believe in making pesto by hand with a large pestle and mortar.) First, crush the garlic, then add the basil leaves plus the oil, and grind to a paste. Add the cheeses and pine nuts, and grind to your desired texture.

2 Cook the potatoes until tender, then drain well. Place the beans in a serving dish.

3 Add the potatoes to the beans. Pour in the pesto and mix well. Stir in salt and pepper if needed. Serve warm or at room temperature.

Pesto made painstakingly by hand is infinitely superior to that made in a food processor. The oils in the basil are released more slowly if you work by hand, so the flavor is better. In a food processor, there seems to be some chemical reaction between the basil and garlic and the stainless-steel blade, which gives a metallic taste to the pesto. We've actually made a direct comparison at the cooking school, tasting one pesto against another, and the hand-ground one wins every time.

CROSTINI DI LENTICCHIE

Lentil Crostini

This appears on every menu in Umbria, and often as part of a mixed plate of crostini, along with a meat spread and a vegetable one. Although made with humble ingredients, the crostini can be served as an elegant starter for a dinner party. The best lentils to use are the *lenticchie di Norcia* (see page 81).

SERVES 4

Lentil Spread

1 tablespoon olive oil

1 small onion, peeled and very finely chopped

4 to 5 fresh sage leaves, finely chopped

1 cup (8 ounces) small green lentils

2¼ cups boiling water

sea salt and freshly ground black pepper

To serve

8 slices slightly stale rustic bread, toasted

a few fresh sage leaves, finely chopped

1 To make the spread, heat the oil in a saucepan until moderately hot, but not smoking. Add the onion and sage, and sauté for 5 minutes.

2 Stir in the lentils and, as soon as they are well coated with oil, pour in the boiling water.

3 Cover and simmer for about 1 hour or until the lentils are soft but still whole. Season with salt and pepper.

4 Spread while warm on the toast slices, and garnish with the chopped sage leaves.

Crostini are very popular in Italy because we always have so much stale bread left over. This is because, when a tax was imposed on salt – around the twelfth century – bakers decided not to use it, and of course bread without salt goes stale very quickly. In fact, in my village, we have to buy bread twice a day.

FAGIOLI ALL'UCCELLETTO

Beans with Tomato Sauce and Sage

This is a typical dish from Tuscany. Its name is derived from *uccelletti,* or "little birds," as the sage leaves resemble little birds' beaks. Another way of enjoying sage is to dip leaves into flour, then into eggs beaten with grated Parmesan, and then fry them until they resemble golden pillows. Serve as an appetizer with drinks.

SERVES 4

¼ cup olive oil

2 tablespoons unsalted butter

3 garlic cloves, peeled and crushed

12 fresh sage leaves, roughly chopped

7 ounces canned chopped tomatoes, or 4 ripe tomatoes, chopped

1 cup (8 ounces) cooked cannellini beans (see page 79)

sea salt and freshly ground black pepper

extra virgin olive oil

1 Heat the oil and butter in a saucepan. Add the garlic and sage and fry gently for 1 minute.

2 Add the tomato and cooked beans, then season with salt and pepper and simmer for 15 minutes.

3 Serve hot with the extra virgin olive oil drizzled on top.

You can burn sage leaves in your home, for cleansing purposes, and for encouraging clarity of mind with less forgetfulness! The name of the herb in English also means wise.

FARINATA

Tuscan Chickpea Polenta

If you keep some chickpea flour in your pantry, this recipe can be a real standby. It makes an interesting accompaniment to other foods – meats or vegetables – and may be pepped up by herbs, more garlic and perhaps some chile. Use your culinary license and experiment!

SERVES 4

6⅓ cups Vegetable Stock
   (page 61) or water
1 pound chickpea flour
sea salt

2 garlic cloves, peeled and
   crushed
6 to 8 tablespoons olive oil
freshly ground black pepper

1 Pour the stock into a large heavy pan, then gradually stir in the flour. Add some salt and the garlic, and cook over low heat for 1 hour, stirring frequently and skimming the surface with a slotted spoon occasionally. It should be smooth and quite thick.

2 Meanwhile, preheat the oven to 400°.

3 Pour the mixture evenly into a 12-inch-square, oiled baking pan. Drizzle the oil over the top. Bake in the preheated oven for 30 minutes until golden brown. Sprinkle liberally with pepper, cut into 2-inch squares, and serve immediately.

The French have a similar dish, called panisse, *also made with chickpea flour. This flour is also used in the Indian subcontinent, where it is known as* gram *or* besan *and is used in the making of many batters and noodles.*

VERDURA

When I am traveling through Italy, mainly by train, it always makes me happy to see back and front gardens, station flower beds, window boxes and terra cotta pots on sunny balconies brimming with bushy tomato plants or rows of basil or oregano. Around midday, one might be lucky enough to catch a glimpse of the cook's deft hand reaching out of a window to pinch a sprig of fresh basil to add to her spaghetti.

This brings home to me, every time, the fact that the Italians were the original market gardeners. Many of the vegetables we are familiar with today were developed in Italy, among them tomatoes, broccoli, fennel, celery and artichokes. The land is still principally utilized for growing, much more than it is for grazing, and as a result the Italians have always been much more interested in vegetables as food and inventive with vegetable recipes. Meat is seen as an expensive commodity, and its consumption in Italy is much less than that in many other Western countries. Vegetables are so important to the Italians, in fact, that they have been given a course in the meal all their own: *contorno*.

The quality of vegetables in Italy is superb, since they are grown for flavor rather than for looks or quantity – and I am not just saying that because my father grows vegetables! How I wish Italian varieties of potato, onion, zucchini and pepper were more widely available in Britain, where I live. They simply taste so much better, and must be healthier than the other available produce, since vegetables grown in Italy tend to be entirely organic.

When it is harvest time, vegetables are treated and cooked very carefully. They are never drowned in a lot of water, or boiled for a great length of time, because this would deprive them of their vitamins. Rather, they are steamed or poached briefly in a small amount of water, or sautéed briskly in some wonderful olive oil with complementary flavorings such as garlic, shallot and/or chile. Green vegetables are added to boiling water with a teaspoon of olive oil, which helps preserve their vibrant color, and a saucepan lid is never used, since this would also cause the color to fade. The cooking water from vegetables is always reserved and used for soups the next day – a healthy practice, since the water contains the nutrients leached from the vegetables.

The recipes in this chapter contain a number of influences, from both north and south. The warmer south is where Mediterranean vegetables such as tomatoes, peppers, zucchini and eggplants flourish, and the local recipes reflect this bounty. Many of the vegetables that are more familiar to those in northern Europe, such as cauliflower, are grown in the colder north.

ZUCCHINI A SCAPECE

Sun-Dried Zucchini with Mint and Garlic

This can be eaten either as a vegetable dish on its own, or as a salad; it's perfect with some good bread. When I make it at the cooking school, we tend to eat it right away, but the marinading intensifies the flavors. The longer it is left, the stronger the flavor will be, but it is so good you won't be able to leave it for very long. I suggest you double the quantities right from the beginning, so you'll be sure to have enough.

SERVES 6

9 large zucchini

¾ cup olive oil

a large handful of fresh mint leaves, coarsely chopped

3 garlic cloves, peeled and finely chopped

6 tablespoons good-quality white wine vinegar

4 tablespoons extra virgin olive oil

sea salt

1 Cut the zucchini into thin slices lengthwise. Place them on a wooden board, cover them with a cloth and leave them in the sun to dry for about 3 hours. Alternatively, put them on a baking sheet in the oven at 275° for about 1 hour to dry out completely without coloring.

2 Heat the oil in a large pan and fry all the dried zucchini slices, in batches if necessary, until golden. Don't bother to turn them over. Drain carefully on paper towels.

3 Transfer the zucchini slices to a dish and sprinkle with the mint, garlic, vinegar, extra virgin olive oil and salt. Cover and let stand in a cool place for about 4 hours or, even better, overnight.

This method of "cooking," called a scapece, is very Neapolitan, and it is often used for fish such as sardines as well as vegetables. Slices of eggplant and strips of sweet pepper can be prepared in the same way.

FAVE CON CIPOLLA ROSSA E FORMAGGIO

Fava Beans Sautéed with Red Onion and Goat Cheese

In the restaurant of a smart hotel outside Rome, I asked if they had fava beans on the menu. Moments later a beautiful platter arrived covered with chunks of ice on which were arranged sheaves of fresh fava beans in the pod. This is how most Italians enjoy fava beans: raw. However, they are also delicious cooked.

SERVES 4

2¼ pounds fava beans in the
   pod, shelled and skinned
1 medium red onion, peeled
   and chopped
2 tablespoons olive oil

sea salt and freshly ground
   black pepper
7 ounces goat cheese
paprika

1 Boil or steam the fava beans until tender, about 10 minutes.

2 Sauté the onion in moderately hot oil for about 5 minutes, then add the hot drained beans, and season to taste. Mix well.

3 Serve in a dish, with thinly sliced goat cheese arranged in a stripe across the top. Sprinkle with paprika.

Skinning fava beans to reveal their bright green inner kernels is immensely time consuming – and rather uneconomical – but it produces a sweeter, much more texturally interesting and visually exciting fava bean.

FAVE AL VINO

Fava Beans with Wine Sauce

On every street corner in the spring you can see groups of little old men passing the time eating young fava beans straight from the pod. This recipe is a way to use fava beans when they are not so young and tender, and cannot be eaten raw.

SERVES 4

2 tablespoons butter

½ onion, peeled and finely chopped

¼ cup all-purpose flour

2¼ pounds fava beans in the pod, shelled

1 sprig fresh marjoram, chopped

sea salt and freshly ground black pepper

1 teaspoon superfine sugar

1¼ cups white wine

⅔ cup Vegetable Stock (page 61)

1 Put the butter in a pan with the onion, and sauté for 4 minutes until golden. Stir in the flour, and cook until you have a thick roux, about 1 minute.

2 Add the beans and the marjoram, salt and pepper to taste, sugar and white wine, and stir to combine.

3 Add the stock, stir, and simmer gently for 20 to 25 minutes, or until the beans are tender.

Being green, fresh fava beans are a good source of vitamin C. You may prefer to remove the outer grayish skin of the beans to reveal the bright green kernels underneath.

MELANZANE CON FUNGHETTI

Eggplant with Tomato and Garlic Sauce

The eggplant is related to the tomato and potato. There are male and female eggplants, as in most of the plant kingdom. Identifiable by its concave base, the male has fewer seeds than the female. As a result, the male has a better flavor, because the seeds can be bitter.

SERVES 4

1 large eggplant, cut into
  1-inch cubes
sea salt
⅔ cup olive oil
2 garlic cloves, peeled and
  crushed

12 ounces tomatoes, skinned
  and chopped
1 tablespoon salted capers,
  rinsed and drained
freshly ground black pepper

1 Put the eggplant in a colander, sprinkle lightly with salt, cover with a small plate, weight down and let stand for 30 minutes. Rinse the eggplant under cold running water, then drain and dry thoroughly.

2 Heat the oil in a heavy sauté pan, add the garlic and fry gently until lightly browned.

3 Add the eggplant and fry for 10 minutes, then add the tomatoes, capers and salt and pepper to taste. Cover and simmer for 30 to 40 minutes, stirring occasionally. Serve hot or cold.

Capers are the flower bud of a shrub native to the Mediterranean. They are available pickled in brine, or salted. The latter are far superior in flavor but, because the buds will have absorbed much of the salt, they need to be thoroughly rinsed before use. Capers in balsamic vinegar and caper buds can occasionally be found.

SCAFATA

Fava Beans with Swiss Chard and Tomato

This is from Piedmont, in the north of Italy, and it is traditionally made with *bietli da taglio*, very young Swiss chard leaves. However, if this is not available, spinach will do.

SERVES 4

4 tablespoons olive oil, fruity and of good quality
1 garlic clove, peeled and crushed
1 onion, peeled and chopped
1 carrot, peeled and diced
1 celery stalk, diced
1 pound 10 ounces fresh fava beans in the pod, shelled
sea salt and freshly ground black pepper

1 pound tender Swiss chard, ribs discarded, leaves cut into strips
1 pound tomatoes, skinned, seeded and finely chopped
a handful of fresh flat-leaf parsley, chopped
a handful of fresh mint, chopped
extra virgin olive oil (optional)

1 Warm the oil in a large saucepan, then add the garlic, onion, carrot, celery and beans, and stir-fry for a few minutes. Add salt and pepper to taste and 4 tablespoons water, cover and cook over a very low heat until the beans are tender. This will depend on their size: if they are young and tender, they will only take about 5 to 7 minutes. If the mixture becomes too dry, add more water.

2 Add the chard and tomato, and cook with the lid partly on until the tomato thickens and the water evaporates.

3 Add the parsley and mint, and add more salt and pepper if necessary. I like to serve this dish slightly warm with some extra virgin olive oil drizzled on top.

Chard and spinach, being dark green in color, are rich in vitamins A and C, and iron. Cook for the least possible time to preserve the C content.

SPINACI ALLA ROMANA

Spinach with Raisins and Pine Nuts

Alla romana means cooking the way people do in Rome. The Romans are very inventive, and this recipe is typical, with pine nuts and raisins to boost the basic flavors of spinach, oil and garlic. Not everyone likes the combination of sweet with savory, but this is really interesting and flavorful.

SERVES 4

2¼ pounds spinach, tough stalks removed
2 tablespoons olive oil
2 tablespoons butter
1 garlic clove, peeled and sliced
2 tablespoons (1 ounce) pine nuts

2 tablespoons seedless raisins, soaked in lukewarm water for 15 minutes and drained
sea salt and freshly ground black pepper

1 Wash (but do not dry) the spinach, then cook in a large pan, with only the water clinging to the leaves, until just tender. Drain well and squeeze out any excess water.

2 Heat the oil and butter in a heavy sauté pan and add the garlic. Fry gently until lightly browned, then discard the garlic.

3 Add the spinach to the oil along with the pine nuts and drained raisins. Cook over medium heat for 10 minutes, stirring frequently, then add salt and pepper to taste. Serve hot.

Any green leafy vegetable is high in vitamins A and C. Dried fruits are a source of nutrients, and the pine nuts, like all nuts, contain many essential fatty acids.

ZUCCA ALL'AGRODOLCE DI PALERMO

Sweet and Sour Pumpkin

I adore pumpkin. This is a typical Sicilian dish, using a sweet spice in a savory context. Many Sicilian recipes use a combination of spices, nuts and dried fruits, an influence from the island's Byzantine past.

SERVES 4

2¼ pounds pumpkin, peeled
  and de-seeded
5 tablespoons olive oil
1 garlic clove, peeled
1 tablespoon granulated sugar

a handful of fresh mint leaves,
  chopped
a pinch of ground cinnamon
8 tablespoons white wine vinegar
freshly ground black pepper

1 Cut the pumpkin flesh into chunks roughly ½ inch thick. In a large frying pan, fry the pumpkin in batches in hot oil with the whole garlic clove for about 3 minutes. Discard the garlic as soon as it browns.

2 When all the pumpkin chunks are fried, place them all back together in the pan, draining off the superfluous oil. Remove from heat.

3 Dredge with sugar, chopped mint and cinnamon. Mix well, then pour the vinegar over, add pepper to taste, cover with the lid, and allow to infuse. Serve warm or cold.

Pumpkins, being yellow fleshed, are rich in beta-carotene. If you save the seeds, you can dry them in a warm oven and eat them as a snack – they are full of zinc, which is particularly good for men.

CARCIOFI CON SPINACI

Artichoke Hearts with Spinach

In Italy, artichokes are sold along the roadside from trucks during artichoke season, which is April, May and October. This recipe comes from the Marche region, famous for delicious artichokes, as well as spinach.

SERVES 4

6 tablespoons olive oil

1 small onion, peeled and finely chopped

1 garlic clove, peeled and crushed

2¼ pounds spinach, washed, drained and finely chopped

¼ cup all-purpose flour

sea salt and freshly ground black pepper

8 young globe artichokes

½ cup dried breadcrumbs

2 ounces Parmesan, freshly grated

a handful of fresh mint, finely chopped

a handful of fresh flat-leaf parsley, chopped

1 Heat half the oil in a large heavy pan, add the onion and garlic, and sauté gently for 5 minutes. Add the spinach and cook for 2 minutes.

2 Stir in the flour and salt and pepper to taste, cover and cook gently for 5 minutes.

3 Preheat the oven to 400°.

4 Clean the artichokes, discarding the hard outer leaves, spikes and chokes (see below). Stand them close together in an oiled ovenproof dish, then cover with the spinach mixture.

5 Scatter with the remaining oil, and the breadcrumbs, Parmesan, pepper and mint. Bake for 20 minutes, then sprinkle with parsley and serve.

Try to buy young artichokes with long, uncut stems. The shorter the stem, the more tough the artichoke tends to be. In young artichokes, the choke will not have developed very much; to remove what "fluff" there is, spread the top leaves, reach in with a teaspoon, and scrape.

CARCIOFI ALLE MANDORLE

Artichoke Hearts with Almond Sauce

This dish is enjoyed in Calabria during artichoke season, using fresh hearts, but you can also use canned. Calabrian dishes are sweet-sour and use a lot of almonds, exhibiting the influence of North Africa.

SERVES 4

Almond sauce

½ red onion, peeled and grated

4 tablespoons olive oil

1 garlic clove, peeled and
    crushed

⅔ cup (4 ounces) ground almonds

1¼ cups Vegetable Stock
    (page 61)

1 tablespoon white wine vinegar

1 tablespoon superfine sugar

juice of 1 lemon

sea salt and freshly ground
    black pepper

6 artichoke hearts, drained (if
    using canned)

2 tablespoons capers, chopped
    (optional)

2 small pickled gherkins,
    chopped (optional)

1 To make the sauce, sauté the onion until golden in 1 tablespoon of the oil, then add the garlic, and allow it to brown lightly. Then stir in the almonds and the stock, and simmer for about 15 minutes, or until thick and creamy.

2 Beat in the remaining oil, the vinegar, sugar, lemon juice and a little salt and pepper, adjusting the quantities to taste. Let cool.

3 Arrange the artichoke hearts on individual plates, pour the sauce over them, and garnish if desired with capers and pickled gherkins. Serve cold.

The wonderfully creamy almond sauce can be served not just with artichokes but with any other cooked vegetable. Because it is completely wheat and dairy free, it is ideal for those with food allergies.

POMODORI AL FORNO

Oven-Baked Tomatoes

I invented this recipe at my home in Italy, in order to use up a glut of tomatoes.
It's great made ahead of time and reheated, but it's good cold as well.

SERVES 4

4 large fresh plum tomatoes

3½ ounces broccoli, cooked
   and chopped

4½ ounces provolone cheese,
   diced

2 tablespoons olive oil

½ garlic clove, peeled and
   crushed

1¾ cups fresh breadcrumbs

a handful of fresh flat-leaf
   parsley, finely chopped

sea salt and freshly ground
   black pepper

1 Core the tomatoes and cut them in half lengthwise. Gently squeeze out some of the juice and pulp. Trim a small piece off the bottom of each tomato half so it will sit without tilting.

2 Place the cut halves in a buttered baking dish large enough to hold them in a single layer. Set aside.

3 Preheat the oven to 350°.

4 In a bowl combine the broccoli and cheese. In a frying pan heat the oil and sauté the garlic lightly. Add the breadcrumbs and parsley, and mix well. Stir the breadcrumb mixture into the broccoli and cheese, and season with salt and pepper.

5 Divide the broccoli mixture evenly over the tomato halves. Bake the tomatoes until the cheese is bubbly and the crumbs begin to brown, about 20 minutes. Serve immediately.

The broccoli and cheese filling could also be used to stuff zucchini, eggplants or onions (the latter would need to be blanched and hollowed out first; see page 135).

INVOLTINI DI MELANZANE

Eggplant Bundles

Involtini are "little rolls," which can be made with many other ingredients, ricotta in place of the mozzarella, for example. The rolls are like eggplant sandwiches, ideal for an antipasto or starter.

SERVES 4

1 medium eggplant
sea salt
6 tablespoons olive oil
1 red bell pepper, roasted and
  skinned (see below)

8 ounces mozzarella cheese,
  sliced lengthwise
a handful of fresh basil leaves
freshly ground black pepper

1 Wash the eggplant and cut off the stem end. Slice lengthwise into ¼-inch-thick slices; you should have about 12. Layer the slices in a colander, sprinkling salt between the layers. Cover with a small plate, weight down and allow to stand for about 30 minutes. Then rinse and pat dry.

2 In a frying pan, heat half the oil, and sauté the eggplant slices in batches (add more oil as needed), keeping them limp. (Do not overcook them, because they would become too brown and would crack.) Drain the eggplant slices on paper towels.

3 Preheat the oven to 400°.

4 Lay each slice of eggplant on a flat surface. Divide the roasted pepper into the same number of portions as you have eggplant slices. Place a portion of pepper on each eggplant slice. Add a slice of mozzarella and a basil leaf, then season each slice with salt and pepper.

5 Roll each eggplant slice up into a cylinder. Place in a lightly oiled baking pan and cover with foil.

6 Heat through in the oven for 10 minutes.

The most successful way to roast a pepper is to place it whole in a baking pan in a 400° oven for 25 minutes. Remove the pepper from the oven and let it cool completely before gently peeling off the skin. Enclosing the pepper in a bag before skinning – as many recipes advise – creates too much steam: the pepper flesh becomes too watery and thus has less firmness.

CIPOLLINE IN AGRODOLCE
Sweet and Sour Onions

This is a typical antipasto dish that is eaten throughout the whole of Italy. It makes a good preserve, covered with olive oil in jars. Of all the dishes I cook at the school, this, one of the simplest, gets the most compliments. It's also a great way of using up the overabundance of grapes in September and October: in fact, for the photograph at right, we picked bunches of sweet and succulent grapes straight from the vines around the school, brought them back to the kitchen, halved them and tossed them immediately in the juices of the onions. Nothing could be more delicious.

Bortonni onions are small and flat, similar to a disc in shape. Native to Italy, they can be quite hard to find elsewhere, but shallots or large scallions will substitute very well.

SERVES 4

½ tablespoon superfine sugar

1 tablespoon butter

2 bay leaves

1 pound *bortonni* onions or
    shallots, peeled

¼ cup white wine

3½ ounces red grapes, halved
    and de-seeded

sea salt and freshly ground
    black pepper

a handful of fresh flat-leaf
    parsley, chopped (optional)

1 Heat the sugar in a heavy pan with a tablespoon of water until it caramelizes and becomes the color of hay. Immediately stir in the butter and bay leaves.

2 Toss the onions into this mixture and cook for a couple of minutes, then pour in the wine. Season, bring to a boil, cover and simmer for 20 minutes.

3 Add the grapes and simmer uncovered for a further 10 minutes, to reduce the liquid. Season with salt and pepper and remove the bay leaves.

4 Pour into a dish and garnish with parsley if desired. Serve hot or cold.

Shallots and onions (and garlic) contain sulphurous chemicals called allins, which are responsible for the onion odor (as well as the tears induced by cutting onions). These are believed in traditional medicine to be tonic, stimulative and diuretic.

FAGIOLI IN PADELLA

"Ratatouille" of Green Beans

This is a specialty of Domodossola, an area in Lombardy in the north of Italy. It is a really tasty bean recipe, and even better if made the day before because all the flavors will have mingled together. I like it as a simple entree served with crusty bread and a salad to follow.

SERVES 4

2 pounds green beans

2 tablespoons olive oil

1 small onion, peeled and chopped

2 garlic cloves, peeled and crushed

2 tablespoons fresh flat-leaf parsley, finely chopped

1 teaspoon fresh basil, or ¼ teaspoon dried basil

¼ cup dry red wine

8 ounces canned or fresh tomatoes and their juices, chopped

sea salt and freshly ground black pepper

1 Remove the ends of the beans, and cut them into 2-inch lengths.

2 Heat the olive oil in a large frying pan and sauté the onion, garlic, parsley and basil for 3 minutes.

3 Add the wine and cook over moderate heat until almost all the wine has evaporated.

4 Add the beans and tomato, season to taste with salt and pepper, and cook gently for 30 minutes or until the beans are tender and the sauce has thickened. Serve hot.

In the north of Italy, people use more alcohol in their cooking than people do in the south. Wine adds flavor and is a great booster to the beans – and to the body! Always use wine that you would drink; please don't compromise on quality when cooking.

CAVOLFIORI DI AMALFI

Parmesan-Fried Cauliflower

This is a family recipe, which can be made with broccoli as well. Do try it, because it will change the way you look at cauliflower.

SERVES 4

1 cauliflower

2 tablespoons all-purpose flour

2 eggs

4 tablespoons freshly grated
    Parmesan

sea salt and freshly ground
    black pepper

a large handful of fresh flat-leaf
    parsley

6 tablespoons olive oil

1 Break the cauliflower into florets, then steam for 6 minutes until tender. Allow to cool completely to room temperature.

2 Coat the cauliflower florets in flour, one at a time.

3 Beat the eggs, then add the Parmesan, and salt and pepper to taste. Finely chop most of the parsley and add it as well.

4 Dip the florets in the egg mixture.

5 Heat the oil in a frying pan and, when hot, fry the cauliflower florets until golden brown on all sides. Drain and serve hot, cold or warm, sprinkled with the remaining parsley leaves.

Make sure the cauliflower is absolutely cooled after cooking, otherwise the batter won't stick. When steaming any brassica, breaking up some bay leaves in the water will neutralize the smell and add the bay's own aroma at the same time.

PEPERONI E PORCINI

Sweet Peppers and Porcini

My friend Claudio gave me this recipe. He has a restaurant called La Taverna in Perugia. This dish is always on his menu, and it is always cooked to perfection.

SERVES 4

3 ounces dried porcini
  mushrooms, reconstituted
  (see page 32)
2 tablespoons olive oil
2 garlic cloves, peeled and
  finely chopped
2 red bell peppers, de-seeded
  and thinly sliced

1 yellow bell pepper, de-seeded
  and thinly sliced
1 medium fennel bulb,
  thinly sliced
sea salt and freshly ground
  black pepper

1 Drain the porcini in a sieve, reserving 2 tablespoons of their soaking water. Dice the porcini.

2 In a medium heavy saucepan, heat the oil and sauté the garlic until soft and just slightly browned.

3 Add the peppers and the fennel, and sauté for 5 minutes, then add the porcini and the reserved soaking water.

4 Cover the saucepan, and simmer for 5 minutes. Season with salt and pepper, and serve at once.

Never throw away porcini soaking water, because it contains so much concentrated flavor. I use it as stock in soups, sauces and risottos.

PEPERONATA

Peppers with Tomato and Onion

This is a classic pepper dish from the south of Italy, where peppers grow in profusion. I think virtually every household has its own "blend." If you put the peperonata in a jar with olive oil to cover, it makes a wonderful present.

SERVES 4

6 tablespoons olive oil

1 onion, peeled and sliced

1 garlic clove, peeled and sliced

2 large red bell peppers, de-seeded and cut into strips

2 large yellow bell peppers, de-seeded and cut into strips

sea salt and freshly ground black pepper

12 ounces tomatoes, skinned and chopped

a handful of fresh flat-leaf parsley, finely chopped

1 Heat the oil in a heavy sauté pan, add the onion and garlic, and cook gently for 5 minutes.

2 Add the peppers, and salt and pepper to taste. Cook for a further 5 minutes, stirring occasionally.

3 Add the tomato and parsley to the peppers. Stir, and add more salt and pepper if needed. Cover and simmer for 20 to 30 minutes, stirring frequently, until thickened. Serve hot or cold as an antipasto.

Peppers are rich in vitamin C, as are tomatoes and parsley. Green bell peppers are unripe and therefore not so sweet as the fully ripe red or yellow bell peppers. Generally speaking, green peppers are not used much in Italian cooking.

ZUCCHINI CON ANICE

Zucchini with Anise Seeds

As soon as I see zucchini in the shops, I know summer is near. Friends in the Veneto gave me this recipe. Usually I cook zucchini with mint, but I was very pleasantly surprised to taste how good they are with anise seeds.

SERVES 4

2 tablespoons best-quality olive oil

2 garlic cloves, peeled and finely minced

½ teaspoon dried red pepper flakes

4 medium zucchini, cut into 2-inch-long matchsticks

1 teaspoon anise seeds

a handful of fresh basil, torn

3 sprigs fresh thyme, finely chopped

sea salt and freshly ground black pepper

2 tablespoons freshly grated Pecorino Romano cheese

1 In a large frying pan heat the olive oil, add the garlic and sauté until soft but not browned.

2 Add the red pepper flakes and zucchini and stir well. Cover and simmer over low heat for 10 minutes.

3 Sprinkle the anise seeds over and cook for 1 minute. Remove from the heat and add the basil, thyme, and salt and pepper to taste. Toss well.

4 Transfer the mixture to a serving dish and sprinkle with the cheese. Serve immediately.

Anise is digestive, and it is used in the making of Sambuca, the famous Italian elderberry liqueur. The anise plant belongs to the same family as dill, caraway and fennel.

FAGIOLINI DI SANT'ANNA

Green Beans in Garlic Sauce

When I'm writing and run short of recipes, my friend Anna from Perugia helps me out – a saint indeed! This is one of her magic recipes: simple, straightforward and delicious.

SERVES 4

3 tablespoons olive oil

2 garlic cloves, peeled and crushed

1 large ripe tomato, skinned and chopped

1¼ pounds green beans, ends removed and halved lengthwise

sea salt and freshly ground black pepper

1 Heat the oil in a medium saucepan, add the garlic and sauté gently until browned. Stir in the tomato and then the beans.

2 Add enough water to barely cover the beans, then add salt and pepper to taste and bring to a boil. Lower the heat, cover, and simmer for 15 to 20 minutes, or until the beans are tender. Toward the end of the cooking time, remove the lid, and increase the heat to reduce the juices. Serve hot or cold.

Green beans are a high-energy food, perfect for those with busy lifestyles.

CIPOLLE FARCITE
Baked Stuffed Onions

These stuffed onions make an ideal *contorno,* a course by themselves. Be inventive with the filling: I recommend this one, but spinach is good, too, and looks wonderful.

SERVES 4

4 onions, peeled

3½ ounces Parmesan, freshly grated

6 tablespoons butter

3 eggs

sea salt and freshly ground black pepper

3 tablespoons brandy

1 Boil onions for 15 minutes in enough water to cover. Drain and cut in half crosswise, then scoop out two-thirds of the flesh with a spoon.

2 Chop the scooped-out flesh and place in a bowl with the cheese, half the butter, the eggs, and salt and pepper to taste. Mix thoroughly, then spoon into the onion shells.

3 Preheat the oven to 400°.

4 Melt the remaining butter on the stove in a flameproof casserole, put the onions in and sprinkle them with the brandy.

5 Bake for 25 minutes, or until golden. Serve right away.

Onions, raw and cooked, contain juices that are antiseptic and good for the whole digestive system.

PATATE AL FORNO

Roasted Potatoes with Garlic, Rosemary and Lemon

These are healthy roasted potatoes, made crispy and flavorful by the lemon juice: the juice caramelizes slightly on the surface starch of the potatoes and turns them golden. The dish is best made with Italian new potatoes, but you can use other varieties, old or new. I make these at the cooking school to accompany fish caught in the nearby lake – a wonderful combination.

SERVES 4

2¼ pounds new potatoes,
   scrubbed
½ cup olive oil
leaves from 1 sprig fresh
   rosemary, finely chopped
juice of 2 lemons

zest of 1 unwaxed lemon,
   grated
3 garlic cloves, peeled and
   finely chopped
sea salt and freshly ground
   black pepper

1 Preheat the oven to 400°.

2 Cut the potatoes into 1-inch cubes. Parboil for 10 minutes, drain and place in a bowl.

3 In a separate bowl, prepare the dressing: whisk together the olive oil, rosemary, lemon juice and zest and the garlic.

4 Pour this dressing over the hot potatoes and toss, then place the potatoes in a roasting pan. Stirring periodically, bake for 25 minutes, or until golden.

5 Season with salt and pepper, and serve warm or cold.

POLPETTE DI PATATE E RICOTTA
Potato and Ricotta Cheese Balls

This Sicilian specialty is very child friendly, since children love to discover the ricotta in the middle. Ricotta is very light and nutritious, and I always keep it in my fridge, because it can be used in so many recipes, both sweet and savory.

SERVES 4

2¼ pounds potatoes, scrubbed

4 eggs

3½ ounces Parmesan, freshly grated

sea salt and freshly ground black pepper

a handful of fresh flat-leaf parsley, chopped

1 cup dried breadcrumbs

2 cups (1 pound) ricotta cheese

1 teaspoon freshly grated nutmeg

olive oil for deep-frying

1 Boil the potatoes in their skins, then peel and mash them. Add 2 of the eggs, the Parmesan, some salt and pepper, the parsley and a handful of the breadcrumbs to thicken the mixture. Blend the ingredients thoroughly.

2 In a bowl, mash the ricotta with a fork. Season with salt and pepper and the nutmeg. Beat the remaining eggs in a small bowl.

3 In your palm dampened with water, make a little nest with the potato mixture, and fill up the hollow with a spoonful of ricotta. Seal with more of the potato mixture to form a ball. Repeat to make more balls.

4 Dip each ball first into the beaten egg, then roll in the remaining breadcrumbs. Deep-fry in the oil until golden. Drain well and serve warm.

These are best eaten in spring when ricotta is at its creamiest and most flavorsome. The milk is at its richest because the sheep have been feeding on the lush green spring grass.

TORTA DI MELANZANA

Eggplant "Cake"

One of my all-time favorites: eggplant, fried in a coating of egg and Parmesan until golden and crispy, then layered with mozzarella cheese and fresh tomato sauce. Ideal for entertaining, it can be made in advance and reheated at the last minute.

SERVES 4

1 medium eggplant, thinly sliced
sea salt
2 pounds fresh ripe tomatoes
6 tablespoons olive oil
1 garlic clove, crushed
1 onion, finely chopped
1 teaspoon sugar

freshly ground black pepper
a handful of fresh basil leaves, torn
2 tablespoons unbleached flour
4 eggs
3 tablespoons freshly grated Parmesan,
  plus extra for sprinkling
12 ounces mozzarella cheese, sliced

1 Sprinkle the eggplant slices with salt, place in a colander, cover with a small plate and weight down. Let stand for 30 minutes.

2 Put the tomatoes in a bowl, cover with boiling water for about a minute, then plunge into cold water. Peel off the skins, then chop the tomatoes.

3 In a large saucepan, heat 2 tablespoons of the oil, add the garlic and sauté until browned, then add the onion and sauté gently until softened. Add the tomato and sugar, bring to a boil, then simmer for 40 minutes, uncovered, to allow the sauce to reduce. Remove from heat, season with salt and pepper and add a few basil leaves. The sauce should be thick and concentrated.

4 Rinse the eggplant and pat dry. Dip the slices in flour and set aside.

5 Whisk the eggs in a bowl and add the 3 tablespoons Parmesan. In a frying pan, heat the remaining oil. Dip the eggplant in the egg mixture and fry until golden on both sides. Drain on paper towels and set aside.

6 Preheat the oven to 375°. Assemble the dish in an 8-inch springform cake pan. Place a layer of the eggplant slices in the bottom. Sprinkle a third of the mozzarella cheese on the eggplant, then spread a third of the tomato sauce on the cheese, and sprinkle a third of the basil leaves on top. Continue adding layers in this order, finishing with a layer of eggplant slices.

7 Sprinkle Parmesan cheese on top and bake for 20 to 25 minutes, or until golden.

Mozzarella can be made from cow's milk, but the genuine cheese is made from buffalo's milk. Mozzarella made in countries other than Italy is usually a poor substitute, often rubbery and without the same melting qualities.

PATATE E ZUCCHINI AL FORNO CON AGLIO

Roasted Potatoes with Zucchini, Garlic and Herbs

Spunta potatoes, which my father grows, are rich and yellow fleshed, with lots of moisture. Even the soil in which they travel – in hand-sewn sacks – smells good! Any potatoes may be used here, but Yukon gold new potatoes are probably the nearest to Spunta.

SERVES 4

6 large new potatoes,
  scrubbed
2 zucchini
6 tablespoons olive oil
3 garlic cloves, peeled and
  crushed into a paste

2 sprigs fresh rosemary,
  chopped
sea salt and freshly ground
  black pepper

1 Preheat the oven to 400°.

2 Cut the potatoes and zucchini into 1-inch chunks. Put the zucchini in a bowl and set aside.

3 In a 13-by-9-inch baking pan, combine the oil and the garlic.

Add the potatoes and coat well with the mixture. Bake for 30 to 45 minutes, basting frequently.

4 Add the zucchini and rosemary to the potatoes, and toss well, then bake for an additional 10 minutes. Sprinkle with salt and pepper and serve at once.

PATATE DELLA NONNA

Grandmother's Potatoes

This reminds me of home – it incorporates two of our firm family favorites: potatoes and spinach. The potato "cake" can be made ahead and reheated. Serve cut in wedges as a *contorno*, a separate vegetable course.

SERVES 4

1 pound new potatoes, peeled

sea salt and freshly ground black pepper

a handful of fresh flat-leaf parsley, finely chopped

½ teaspoon freshly grated nutmeg

3½ ounces Parmesan, freshly grated

2 large eggs, beaten

8 ounces spinach, washed and finely chopped

¼ cup unsalted butter

1 cup fresh breadcrumbs, toasted

1 Boil the potatoes until soft, then drain and mash. Add salt, pepper, parsley, nutmeg, Parmesan, eggs and spinach, and mix well.

2 Preheat the oven to 400°.

3 Grease a 10-inch cake pan with some of the butter, then cover the bottom with half the breadcrumbs. Spread the potato mixture on top, and cover with the remaining breadcrumbs. Dot with the remaining butter.

4 Bake until golden, about 10 minutes.

Italians use a lot of breadcrumbs in cooking. We tend to dry pieces of stale bread in a moderately heated (300°) oven until very brittle, then crush them with a rolling pin. They are stored in an airtight jar and used when needed.

INSALATE

In my family, one of the courses that my grandmother served, every lunchtime, was a salad. She insisted that eating an *insalata* after the main course aided digestion, a healthy way to settle the stomach. She – like many Italians – preferred bitter greens that are called *cicoria*, a term for many varieties of wild and cultivated greens. (Dandelion leaves, for instance – perhaps the wild ancestor of the *cicoria* family – are picked for salads. They have a bitter flavor and are valued for their high iron content.)

I really relish the salad course in the Italian diet, and I love the simplicity of the dressing as well: often just a very good extra virgin olive oil mixed with lemon juice (occasionally balsamic or wine vinegar) and salt and pepper. Even the dressing for salads can contribute to health, for olive oil is monounsaturated, and therefore it doesn't raise your blood cholesterol levels as other oils might. And, of course, it contains many nutrients, comes from organically grown fruit, and is produced in a noncommercial, natural way. When making olive oil dressings, or sprinkling oil onto a dish, use an extra virgin oil. Its taste is magnificent and it varies from region to region – lighter in the north, heavier in the south – but all are unique and exciting. Never cook with extra virgin olive oil: that would be a waste of what I call "green gold."

When making leaf salads, there are a few basic rules to follow: Do not buy limp lettuce or lettuce that has yellow leaves or dark brown spots, an indication of old age. Fresh lettuce is uniformly green and almost stands up on its own. The leaves are springy and squeaky when shaken, and the head should feel solid. The same applies to the so-called "designer leaves," among them arugula, radicchio and *frisée*. Never wash any salad leaves until you are just ready to make the salad. Drain the leaves thoroughly in a colander, then gently roll them in paper towels to absorb excess water (or use a salad spinner). If the lettuce is wet, the oil will not adhere to it. Dress the salad at the last minute.

Of course they don't use only leaves in salads in Italy, and there are many vegetable salads, once again revealing the Italian love for vegetables of all kinds. I have included a wide selection here – among them artichokes, fennel, eggplant and potatoes – and hope you will enjoy them. It is said that a good salad should contain a root, fruit and shoot for a perfect balance of nutrients: I think you'll find that most of the following adhere to this formula to a certain extent.

INSALATA DI MELANZANE E CIPOLLE

Eggplant, Potato and Onion Salad

This recipe came from a family friend in Calabria, Salvatore Veltri. One hot summer, I spent 10 days learning how to cook delicious red onions, which he grows for export. The *Tropea* onion is picked in early spring and late summer, and its bulbs are intensely violet, and round, oval or long. They are sweet and fleshy, and eminently suitable for salads and raw dishes.

SERVES 4

1 firm eggplant, weighing about 7 ounces

sea salt and freshly ground black pepper

7 ounces new potatoes

2 red onions, peeled

a handful of fresh mint leaves

a handful of fresh oregano

1 to 2 tablespoons white wine vinegar

3 tablespoons extra virgin olive oil

sea salt and freshly ground black pepper

1 Peel and wash, then boil the entire eggplant for 10 minutes in plenty of boiling water. Drain and cool. Cut it up into strips and place on a plate.

2 Peel, slice and boil the potatoes until tender. Drain and add to the eggplant.

3 Finely chop the onions and add to the eggplant and potato, along with the herbs, vinegar and oil. Season with salt and pepper, and mix well. Serve at room temperature.

Lino Businco, teacher of general pathology at Rome University, defines onions as "friends of the blood, keeping it as fluid and fluent as the blood of a young man."

INSALATA DI RUCOLA E FICHI

Arugula and Fig Salad

Arugula is a member of the same family as mustard and cress, which is obvious when you bite into it and encounter its bitter, sharp and peppery flavor. It was once cultivated in Britain, but it went out of fashion for centuries until very recently, when Italian imports caused a happy renaissance. Now arugula is the leaf of the moment, appearing in many of the most fashionable salads; it can also be used to make an extremely pungent pesto.

SERVES 4

8 ounces arugula leaves

4½ ounces fresh figs, quartered

1 tablespoon freshly squeezed lemon juice

2 to 3 tablespoons fruity extra virgin olive oil

sea salt and freshly ground black pepper

1 Wash the arugula well, tear into rough pieces, and dry it thoroughly.

2 Toss the quartered figs with the leaves, and add the lemon juice, oil and salt and pepper to taste. Serve at once.

148

INSALATA DI SICILIA

Tomato, Mint and Red Onion Salad

I have very fond memories of eating this salad in Syracuse, Sicily, with my father. Some family friends there grew lettuces, and this salad is what we ate – part of a wonderful meal – after a long dusty drive to their farm. It was the first time I had seen tomatoes, onion and mint together – and it is a stunning combination.

SERVES 4

4 firm, bright-red tomatoes
½ small red onion, peeled and finely
  chopped
a handful of fresh mint, finely chopped
3 tablespoons extra virgin olive oil
juice and zest, finely chopped, of
  1 unwaxed lemon
sea salt and freshly ground black pepper

1 Slice the tomatoes and arrange on a large, plain plate.

2 Sprinkle the onion and mint over the tomatoes, and then drizzle with oil and lemon juice. Sprinkle the lemon zest on top, and season with salt and pepper.

3 Allow the salad to marinate for 20 minutes, and then serve.

All the ingredients must be of the very best quality. When tomatoes are not in season locally, do choose tomatoes that have been grown in a sunny country, so that some of the goodness of the southern sun will have sweetened the flesh and produced a beautiful ripe tomato with a deep red skin.

BROCCOLI IN INSALATA

Broccoli Salad

The Italian love of vegetables is amply illustrated by the fact that they even eat broccoli in a salad. A crispness comes from the raw carrot, a softer texture from the cooked broccoli. The lemon juice recognizably enhances the flavor of the broccoli, just as it does many other cooked green vegetables (particularly chard, one of my favorite vegetables).

SERVES 4

1 pound broccoli florets
sea salt
4 small carrots
juice of 4 lemons
½ teaspoon dried red pepper flakes
freshly ground black pepper
2 tablespoons fruity olive oil

1 Cook the broccoli florets in boiling, salted water for 7 minutes. Drain and plunge into cold water to prevent further cooking. Drain again and leave to cool.

2 Scrape the carrots and shred them into thin strips.

3 Combine the carrots and cold broccoli, and dress with lemon juice, red pepper flakes, salt and pepper to taste, and oil.

Broccoli is a type of flowering cabbage developed in Calabria, hence its other name, calabrese. Buy broccoli when it is bright green, not yellow. Look at the stalk end, which ought to appear as if newly cut; if it looks dry, the broccoli could be tough. Broccoli, being green, contains vitamins A and C as well as many minerals. You could also try purple sprouting broccoli, which has a delicious, nutty flavor.

151

INSALATA DI RINFORZO

Cauliflower Salad

The Italian name of this dish means "reinforced salad," because it is served at Christmas to "back up" or "reinforce" the other dishes on the table, acting as a refreshing interlude between courses.

SERVES 4

1 cauliflower

sea salt

2 ounces green olives, halved and pitted

1 tablespoon good-quality capers

1 tablespoon chopped sun-dried tomatoes

1 red pepper, roasted (see page 123), skinned and finely chopped

a handful of fresh flat-leaf parsley, finely chopped

freshly ground black pepper

2 tablespoons extra virgin olive oil

2 tablespoons red wine vinegar

1 Cut the cauliflower into small, uniform florets. Rinse well in cold water and drain. Put the florets in a large pot and add cold water to cover. Add 1 teaspoon salt and bring to a boil. Boil the cauliflower until al dente, 5 to 6 minutes, then drain.

2 Meanwhile, in a salad bowl, combine the olives, capers, sun-dried tomatoes, roasted pepper, parsley and salt and pepper to taste. Then add the cooked cauliflower.

3 In a small bowl, whisk together the oil and vinegar. Add to the vegetables and toss well. Cover the bowl and leave the salad to marinate in a cool place for about an hour before serving.

Cauliflower in Italy is at its best in the winter and is featured frequently in cooking in December. Olives too will just have been harvested, often used for the first time at the Christmas dinner table.

INSALATA DI SPINACI E PATATE

Spinach and Potato Salad

The combination of these two ingredients is rather delicious, creating a salad that is warming and satisfying, with a meaty texture. Since these two vegetables are commonly cooked together in the Indian subcontinent, perhaps Marco Polo had a hand in bringing the idea to Europe.

SERVES 4

2¼ pounds spinach

¼ cup unsalted butter

sea salt and freshly ground black pepper

3 tablespoons extra virgin olive oil

½ tablespoon balsamic vinegar

4 new potatoes, scrubbed and thinly sliced

1 Wash the spinach well (but do not dry) and remove any tough stems. Cook in a large pan, with only the water clinging to the leaves, until wilted.

2 Add the butter to the spinach along with some salt and pepper and the oil and vinegar. Toss until all the spinach leaves are coated.

3 Boil the potato slices until tender and toss into the spinach. Serve warm.

This is a good salad to serve in the winter, containing the carbohydrate of the potato and the nutrients of the green vegetable.

CARCIOFI CON PESTO

Artichoke Salad with Pesto

I have already given a pesto recipe, but this one is different, using less basil and garlic. This is because the artichokes have such a special flavor, and I didn't want the pungency of those two ingredients to overpower it.

SERVES 4

6 baby artichokes
juice of 2 lemons

Pesto
2 ounces fresh basil leaves
3 tablespoons extra virgin
**   olive oil**

1 garlic clove, peeled and
**   crushed**
3 tablespoons freshly grated
**   Parmesan**
1 tablespoon freshly grated
**   Pecorino Romano cheese**
2 tablespoons pine nuts

1 To prepare the artichokes, snap back the tough leaves and pull down, working your way around the layers. Stop when you get to the pale yellow, tender leaves. Cut off the tops of the remaining leaves, leaving about 1 inch of leaf.

2 Use a paring knife to trim away the dark green areas along the base. Trim off the base of the stem end and cut away the tough fibers around the stem end, leaving just the light-colored, tender center portion. Cut the artichokes in half lengthwise. Using a paring knife, carefully cut away the fuzzy choke, trying to cut just at the point where choke and heart meet. Set in a pot in acidulated water to cover, i.e., water with the lemon juice added. Bring to a boil, without lid.

3 Boil the artichokes for 10 minutes if small, a bit longer if larger. Drain and leave to cool.

4 To make the best pesto (see also page 99), use a large pestle and mortar to grind all the ingredients together slowly by hand until a smooth paste is formed.

5 Pour the pesto over the artichokes, and serve at room temperature.

If fresh artichokes aren't available, you can use fresh artichoke hearts – or canned hearts that have been drained, then marinated in extra virgin olive oil with a little garlic.

INSALATA DI PEPERONI E CAPPERI

Pepper Salad with Capers

This salad always seemed to be available in the kitchen when hunger struck in my childhood. All we needed to do for an emergency snack was cut a substantial hunk of bread and top it with the salad and its juices.

SERVES 4

3 yellow bell peppers, roasted (see page 123), skinned and de-seeded
4 large ripe tomatoes
1 medium garlic clove, peeled
a handful of fresh basil leaves, torn
a handful of fresh mint leaves, torn
2 tablespoons extra virgin olive oil
sea salt and freshly ground black pepper
2 tablespoons best-quality capers in balsamic vinegar

1 Cut the peppers into thin strips. Cut the tomatoes into pieces. Finely chop the garlic and combine with the tomato in a bowl. Add the basil, mint, oil, and salt and pepper to taste, and mix very well.

2 Arrange the pepper strips on a serving dish and pour the prepared tomato "sauce" over them. Toss well, and leave to infuse for 30 minutes.

3 Serve sprinkled with the capers, and some extra mint leaves if desired.

Tomatoes and basil are often grown together – companion planting – because the fragrant oils of the basil help keep aphids and other insects away from the tomatoes. Thus it seems entirely natural that they should be eaten together.

INSALATA DI FINOCCHIO E ARANCIA

Fennel and Orange Salad

This Sicilian salad is colorful and unusual, and packed full of vitamin C. A traditional story tells that when there is nothing to eat in Sicily there are always blood oranges, so called because of their deep red color.

SERVES 4

6 medium blood oranges or navel oranges
1 medium fennel bulb, trimmed and cut into thin strips
2 tablespoons finely minced fennel leaves
3 tablespoons finely chopped fresh walnuts
2 tablespoons fruity extra virgin olive oil
sea salt and freshly ground black pepper
8 romaine lettuce leaves

1 Peel the oranges and remove as much of the pith as possible. Slice the oranges into thin rounds and place them in a shallow dish, slightly overlapping.

2 Sprinkle the fennel strips, fennel leaves and walnuts on top. Drizzle with the oil and sprinkle with salt and pepper.

3 Cover and let stand at room temperature for several hours. Every so often, tilt and turn the salad so that the oil and juices that have collected flow over and around the oranges.

4 To serve, arrange the salad on a bed of lettuce leaves, and pour the juices over the salad.

This illustrates the sweet and sour flavors that are so prevalent in the south. The acidity comes from the blood oranges – they are more tangy than navels – and the sweetness from the fennel.

INSALATA CON ERBE

Green Salad with Wild Herbs

This recipe comes from the deeply religious south of the country, where every facet of life seems to be analyzed or dissected in terms of superstition or religion. Here we use seven herbs for the seven cardinal virtues.

SERVES 4

1 head crisp, fresh romaine lettuce

½ Treviso radicchio

a handful of arugula leaves

a large handful in total of 7 wild herbs from the garden (i.e., basil, parsley, thyme, marjoram, chives, sage and mint), finely chopped together

1 fennel bulb, thinly sliced

Dressing

3 tablespoons best-quality extra virgin olive oil

1 tablespoon freshly squeezed lemon juice

sea salt and freshly ground black pepper

1 Wash and pat dry all the salad leaves. In a bowl, mix the leaves and herbs together, and then toss in the fennel slices.

2 Combine the oil and lemon juice, seasoning to taste with salt and pepper.

3 To preserve the crispness of the leaves, dress the salad immediately before serving.

INSALATA D'ORTO

Garden Salad

This is an invention of mine that came about simply through opening the fridge and seeing what was there. It's full of texture and flavor, and it looks good as well.

SERVES 4

2 celery stalks

2 carrots, peeled

1 small red onion, peeled

8 small vine-ripened tomatoes

a handful of fresh flat-leaf parsley

a handful of fresh mint

3 tablespoons fruity extra virgin olive oil

1 tablespoon lemon juice

sea salt and freshly ground black pepper

1 Coarsely chop the celery, carrots and onion. Cut the tomatoes in half. Finely chop the parsley and mint.

2 Put all the ingredients in a bowl, and season to taste with salt and pepper. Mix together and serve at once.

Celery should be enjoyed when yellow, not green. The flavor is superior, more mellow, since it has had time to mature. Celery has great digestive properties, being highly alkaline. (This is why it is often served with cheese, which is acidic.)

INSALATA DELLA NONNA

Grandmother's Special Salad

This hearty salad is full of goodness. The combination of beans and potatoes also makes it a filling snack.

SERVES 4

1 pound green beans, cut into bite-sized pieces
1 pound new potatoes, boiled
2 tablespoons freshly squeezed lemon juice
4 tablespoons extra virgin olive oil
sea salt and freshly ground black pepper
1 handful of freshly chopped oregano
1 clove garlic, finely crushed
12 cherry tomatoes, preferably vine-ripened, cut in half

1 Steam the beans for approximately 7 minutes, or until tender.

2 Cook the potatoes in boiling salted water for 10 to 15 minutes, depending on their size, or until tender.

3 While the beans and potatoes are cooking, mix the lemon juice and oil together with the salt and pepper, herbs and garlic.

4 Add the tomatoes to the dressing and toss with the potatoes and beans.

I have a huge passion for extra virgin olive oil. It is worth experimenting with different oils – in the same way many people try wines – to find one that you particularly like. The best are dark green and strong in flavor. Remember that price is usually a good indication of quality.

PANZANELLA ALLA MINORI

Bread, Onion and Tomato Salad

There are many variations of this salad, which originates in Tuscany. It is a bread salad created, like so many other Tuscan dishes, to utilize left-over stale bread. In this context, bread mops up all the delicious juices of the vegetables, and really is a bonus – especially when you have a large number of mouths to feed.

SERVES 4

7 ounces rustic white bread, crusts removed
5 tomatoes, preferably vine-ripened, finely chopped
1 red onion, peeled and finely chopped
½ cucumber, finely chopped
2 celery stalks, finely chopped
6 black olives, pitted and chopped
a handful of fresh basil, torn
a handful of fresh mint, coarsely chopped
⅓ cup extra virgin olive oil
2 tablespoons white wine vinegar
sea salt and freshly ground black pepper

1 Cut the bread into chunks, and put them in a salad bowl and sprinkle with 1 tablespoon water.

2 Add all the vegetable and herb ingredients, and toss.

3 Dress with the oil and vinegar, and season with salt and pepper. Toss, and allow to marinate for half an hour before serving.

An open-textured bread – one made with olive oil – is best, because it holds its shape and does not disintegrate. A store-bought ciabatta, or the olive bread on page 166, would be good.

PANE

Most cultures throughout the world have a tradition of bread-making, and it is particularly strong in Italy. No Italian meal is complete without bread, and no Italian cook worth his or her salt would ever offer food without the accompaniment of some sort of bread. Its inclusion in a meal is automatic, as much a part of laying the table as arranging the cutlery and folding the napkins.

At an ordinary meal, Italians might eat a rustic, plain type of risen bread, one with an open texture, probably made with olive oil: a ciabatta, perhaps, or a *Pugliese* bread, made with semolina and hard wheat, from Puglia in southern Italy (which lasts longer than most other Italian breads). But many breads can have other ingredients baked within them, like the cheese and olive breads in the pages following. Some breads are made rolled around a filling, and others are baked flat, to hold a topping. The pizza from Naples is perhaps the most familiar, but there are variations all over Italy: the focaccia or hearth bread of Genoa and elsewhere, and the *schiacciata* of Emilia-Romagna. Breads can be savory, or sweet (which are wonderful served for breakfast), and there are also many festive breads, made traditionally at times of religious significance or celebration, such as Easter and Christmas.

Italian breads go stale quite quickly, often because they are baked without salt, which acts as a preservative. This is particularly so in Tuscany, where a heavy salt tax in the Middle Ages led bakers to devise bread recipes that did not require salt. As a result, there are many recipes in the Tuscan culinary canon that utilize stale bread: bread soup, or *pappa al pomodoro;* and *panzanella,* a bread salad (see page 159). Bread is also made into *crostini,* or croutons; *bruschetta,* with its drizzled topping of olive oil (or something more ambitious); and breadcrumbs, an important ingredient in many regional cuisines.

I bake bread several times a week, and I eat it every day. It represents a significant part of my diet, because it is a complex carbohydrate, releasing energy slowly into the body. If I eat bread at a meal, to accompany a salad or vegetable dish, this healthy combination will keep me going well until the next mealtime, and I won't be tempted to have a less-than-healthy snack.

Something wonderful happens to your kitchen and your life when bread making becomes a regular activity: the fragrance and suspense of it; the sharing of its warmth and goodness when it comes out of the oven; the very fact that we care enough to take the time – all these remind us that home is a fine place to be. Though perhaps a small thing, bread making to me seems like a counterweight to the forces pulling family and friends apart. In fact, bread making is the one culinary activity I get really passionate about, and I think it would be a wonderful thing to encourage children to participate in, allowing their sense of achievement and pride to begin.

BIGA

Italian Bread Starter

I believe this to be the cornerstone of great Italian bread. Wheat in Italy is traditionally poor for bread making, so *bigas* were designed to boost and enhance the performance of breads, just as a turbo enhances the performance of a car (a simile coined by one of my students). A *biga* gives the bread those "eyes," the wonderful open texture, and the deep delicious smell to the dough. It can be incorporated at the beginning stage of any bread: add ¼ cup of the *biga* to the well in the flour when you are adding the liquid, foaming yeast.

⅛ ounce fresh yeast, or ¼ teaspoon active dry

⅔ cup warm water

1 cup plus 2 tablespoons unbleached flour

1 Crumble the yeast into the water in a bowl, add the flour and stir to form a thick batter.

2 Cover with a damp dishcloth, and leave to ferment at room temperature for 24 to 36 hours before use, but no longer, since it will get tangier and sourer. Keep the cloth damp.

Please note that you will still have to add yeast to your recipe, even if you are using a biga. *And if you find there is slight separation in the* biga, *don't be alarmed; simply stir it all back together.*

PANE DI OLIVE

Olive Bread

I found this recipe when I was on a food-tasting trip in Liguria, and of the many olive breads I tried, this was my favorite. Do use the best olives you can, preferably the ones preserved in oil, since these have far more flavor. You may have to spend quite a while pitting the olives, but it will all be worth it! And once you have mastered this bread recipe, you could show your creativity by adding an herb: thyme or oregano would be good.

MAKES 4 SMALL LOAVES

½ ounce fresh yeast, or
   2 teaspoons active dry
1 cup warm water
4 cups unbleached flour

½ teaspoon sea salt
4 tablespoons olive oil
5½ ounces black olives,
   pitted and chopped

1 In a small bowl, combine the yeast and ¼ cup of the water. Cover and let stand until frothy, about 15 minutes.

2 Put the flour and salt in a large mixing bowl together with 3 tablespoons of the olive oil. Pour the frothy yeast into the flour along with most of the remaining water, and work it into a stiff, sticky dough. Add the remaining water if necessary.

3 Knead for about 10 minutes or until the dough is smooth and elastic, adding a little more flour if necessary. Add the olives and knead them into the dough.

4 Put another tablespoon of oil into the bowl and turn the dough in it to grease the surface and prevent any crust from forming. Cover the bowl with a damp cloth and let the dough rise in a warm place for about 1½ hours, or until doubled in bulk.

5 Knead the dough again for a few minutes, then divide into four balls. Place the balls on an oiled baking sheet. Press them down gently, or shape them in any way you like. Let the dough rise again, covered, for 1 hour.

6 Preheat the oven to 475°.

7 Brush the loaves with water to soften the crust, and bake for about 30 minutes. Cool on wire racks.

Olive oil is a monounsaturated fat, and olives therefore are a storehouse of this substance. Olives contain many minerals, as well as vitamins A and E. Green olives are more astringent than black, and small olives are usually more intense in flavor than large ones. Experiment!

FOCACCIA DI LIGURIA CON FONTINA

Ligurian Bread with Potato and Fontina Cheese

Focaccia can be thick or thin, depending on the part of Italy you are in – often fashionably thin in the elegant north and fatter in the more rustic south. This particular focaccia is very thin, topped with potato slices arranged like fish scales, and the local mountain Fontina cheese. It is good, warming winter food.

SERVES 8

¼ ounce fresh yeast, or
  1 teaspoon active dry
1½ cups warm water
7 tablespoons *Biga*
  (page 165)
3 tablespoons extra virgin
  olive oil
4 cups unbleached flour
1½ teaspoons sea salt

Topping

9 ounces new potatoes, scrubbed
  and thinly sliced
sea salt
2 garlic cloves, peeled and crushed
4½ ounces fontina cheese,
  sliced, rind removed
1 to 2 teaspoons olive oil
freshly ground black pepper
4 teaspoons finely chopped
  fresh rosemary

1 Whisk the yeast into the warm water in a large mixing bowl, and add the *biga* and olive oil. In a separate bowl, combine the flour and salt, then stir into the yeast mixture to form a soft dough.

2 Turn the dough onto a floured surface and knead for 8 to 10 minutes, or until smooth and elastic. Place in a lightly oiled bowl, cover with plastic wrap, and leave to rise for 1 to 1½ hours, or until doubled in size.

3 Meanwhile, for the topping, blanch the potato slices in salted water for 5 minutes, then drain and dry. Set aside.

4 Turn the dough out of the bowl and press into an 18-by-13-inch baking sheet, forming the dough into an oval shape.

5 Dimple the dough with your fingertips and spread with the garlic, potatoes, cheese, olive oil and some salt and pepper. Finish by sprinkling the rosemary over the top. Let stand for 20 minutes at room temperature.

6 Meanwhile, preheat the oven to 400°.

7 Bake the bread for 25 to 30 minutes, or until the top is golden. Cool on a wire rack and eat while still warm.

Make sure you use good potatoes: Italian new potatoes, such as Spunta or Elvira, are delicious and occasionally can be found in supermarkets. However, any waxy new potato from a hot country with good soil can be substituted.

PANE CON POMODORI E CIPOLLE ROSSE

Tomato and Red Onion Bread

This robustly flavored loaf originated in Tropea, located in southern Italy's Calabria region, where tomatoes and onions flourish, and strong, peppery dishes are favored.

MAKES 1 LOAF

1 ounce fresh yeast, or 4 teaspoons
  active dry

⅔ cup warm water

4 cups unbleached flour

2 teaspoons sea salt

1 pound ripe tomatoes

1 tablespoon olive oil

2 red onions, peeled, halved and
  finely sliced

1 tablespoon chopped fresh
  oregano

1 teaspoon dried red pepper flakes

1 Dissolve the yeast in the warm water in a bowl. Let stand for 5 minutes, then stir. Combine the flour and salt in a large bowl. Make a well in the center of the flour and pour in the yeasted water.

2 Using a wooden spoon, gradually draw enough of the flour into the yeasted water to form a thick paste. Cover the bowl with a dishcloth and leave to "sponge" until frothy and risen, about 1 hour.

3 Skin the tomatoes by immersing them in boiling water for 1 minute. Score the skin with a knife and peel it away. Remove and discard the cores and seeds, and roughly chop the flesh.

4 Heat the olive oil in a sauté pan, then add the tomatoes, onions, oregano and red pepper flakes. Cover the pan and cook gently for 10 minutes. Transfer the tomato mixture to a bowl and leave to cool.

5 Stir the cooled tomato mixture into the fermented sponge mix in the flour to make a soft, sticky dough. Pull in more flour if the dough is too wet to handle.

6 Turn the dough out onto a lightly floured work surface. Knead until silky and supple, about 10 minutes.

7 Put the dough in a lightly oiled bowl and cover with a damp dishcloth. Allow to rise until doubled in size, about 1 hour. Punch down, then chafe for 5 minutes (see below). Allow to rest for a further 10 minutes.

8 Shape the dough into a round loaf. Place on an oiled baking sheet, cover and leave until doubled in size, about 35 minutes. Preheat the oven to 400°. Bake for 45 minutes, or until golden and hollow-sounding when tapped on bottom. Cool on a wire rack.

To "chafe," apply a light downward pressure to the sides of the round ball of dough, while simultaneously rotating the dough continuously in a steady clockwise motion. This lightens the bread, giving it more bubbles.

CRESCIA

Cheese and Black-Pepper Bread

This is an old family recipe, and I was very excited to see it in a Roman bakery recently (Volpetti in Testaccio). It is very, very tasty because of the rich, strong cheese and the spicy pepper. Serve it with wine and some fruit.

MAKES 1 LOAF

¼ **cup warm water**

½ **ounce fresh yeast, or**
   2 teaspoons active dry

¼ **cup warm whole milk**

3 **large eggs**

6 **ounces Pecorino Romano**
   cheese, cubed

½ **tablespoon coarsely ground**
   black pepper

¾ **cup unsalted butter,**
   melted and slightly cooled

4 **cups unbleached flour**

1 **tablespoon olive oil**

1. Place the water in a small bowl, sprinkle the yeast over it, and stir to dissolve. Let the yeast activate, covered, for about 10 minutes, or until foamy. Add the milk.

2. In a large bowl beat the eggs with a whisk until well blended, then add the yeast mixture. Stir in the cheese, pepper and melted butter, then the flour, a bit at a time, until a soft ball of dough is formed. Add more flour if the dough is sticky.

3. Turn the dough out onto a floured work surface and knead until it is consistent in texture and feels silky to the touch, about 5 minutes. Let the dough rest, covered with a dishcloth, on a floured surface for 10 minutes.

4. Pour the olive oil into a large bowl, place the dough in the bowl and turn to grease it. Cover the bowl with a dishcloth and leave the dough to rise until doubled in size, about 1½ hours.

5. Punch the dough down, place on a lightly floured work surface, and knead into a smooth ball. Place the bread on a greased baking sheet, and allow to rise for 30 minutes.

6. Meanwhile, preheat the oven to 400°.

7. Bake the bread for 30 to 35 minutes, or until nicely browned. Cool on a wire rack.

This bread can be made in a ring shape as well, or even rolls (but bake rolls for less time). As a general rule, the more you knead, the less flavor a bread will have, but, ironically, every bread does actually need to be kneaded.

CALZONE DI PREZZEMOLO

Folded Parsley Pizza

The literal translation of *calzone* is "trouser leg," referring to the double thickness of fabric or, in this case, bread dough. The recipe comes from the Bar Mundial in Cassibile, Sicily (thank you, Gianni Fronterrè). It is lighter than you might expect, not as doughy as many other calzoni, and the filling, despite being incredibly simple, is quite delicious.

MAKES 1 LARGE CALZONE

¼ ounce fresh yeast, or
   1 teaspoon active dry
a little superfine sugar
1 cup warm water
5 cups unbleached flour
1 tablespoon sea salt
⅓ to ½ cup olive oil

1 onion, peeled and finely
   chopped
a very large handful of fresh
   flat-leaf parsley, chopped
freshly ground black pepper
12 ounces mozzarella
   cheese, cut into small cubes
all-purpose flour for dusting

1. In a small bowl, combine the yeast with the sugar and add a little of the water. Let the yeast activate for about 10 minutes, or until foamy.

2. Combine the flour and salt in a large bowl. Add half the oil and the yeast mixture, together with the remaining water. Stir with a wooden spoon to form a dough.

3. Turn the dough out of the bowl onto a floured work surface and knead vigorously for 10 minutes, until soft and pliable. Return the dough to a clean bowl. Cover with a cloth and allow to rise until doubled in size, about 1 hour.

4. Meanwhile, prepare the filling by heating the remaining oil in a sauté pan. Sauté the onion until soft, then add the parsley and cook, stirring for 2 minutes over medium heat. Season with pepper and set aside. When cool, stir in the cheese.

5. Preheat the oven to 400°.

6. Punch down the dough and knead for 4 minutes. Roll out into a large rectangle 15 by 8 inches. Spread the onion and cheese mixture over the dough, leaving a ½-inch margin all round.

7. Now fold the dough over lengthwise in three parts, enclosing the filling, seal the ends, and place on a greased baking sheet. Allow to rise again for 10 minutes and then dust with a little flour.

8. Bake for 20 minutes, or until light and golden. Cool on a wire rack and then cut into thick or thin slices, for snacks or canapés. Serve hot, cold or warm!

You can change the filling, using other cheeses, or even meats. Try to use flat-leaf parsley, though, which is more intense in flavor than curly.

173

FOCACCIA ALL'OLIO E SALVIA

Sage and Olive Oil Bread

It's difficult to have too much of this delicate-tasting, light and porous bread, which is made with water, wine and olive oil. It is made by the sponge method, which is a quicker version of *biga*, for when you want to have flavor and texture in a shorter time. The use of the wine may be unusual, but it acts as an extra ferment and adds a deeper flavor. The sage on the top becomes crispy in the oven and looks and tastes marvelous.

SERVES 4

Sponge

¾ ounce fresh yeast, or
   2½ teaspoons active dry
½ cup warm water
1⅓ cups unbleached flour

Dough

⅓ cup dry white wine
⅓ cup light olive oil
20 fresh sage leaves, chopped
½ ounce fresh yeast, or
   2 teaspoons dry
1 tablespoon warm water
3 cups unbleached flour
2 teaspoons sea salt

Topping

2 tablespoons good-
   quality olive oil
1 to 2 teaspoons sea salt
4 fresh sage leaves

1 To make the sponge, sprinkle the yeast over the warm water in a large mixing bowl, whisk it in and let it stand until creamy, about 10 minutes. Stir in the flour and beat until smooth. Cover tightly with plastic wrap and leave it to rise until puffy and bubbling, about 30 minutes.

2 To make the dough, add the wine, oil, sage and yeast (activated in warm water) to the sponge mixture, then whisk in the flour and salt, just a little at a time, until the dough is very soft and sticky. Knead on a lightly floured surface, adding more flour if necessary. It should be soft but not wet.

3 Place the dough in a lightly oiled container, cover tightly, and let rise for 20 minutes.

4 Punch the dough down, and roll out to a circle about ¼ inch thick. Place on an oiled baking sheet, cover and let rise for 1 hour.

5 At least 30 minutes before you plan to bake, preheat the oven to 400°. If you have one, put a baking stone in the oven.

6 Dimple the top of the bread with your fingertips. Drizzle with the oil and sprinkle with salt and sage.

7 Place the bread in the well preheated oven (on the baking stone if appropriate). Spray the oven with cold water from a spritzer 3 times during the first 10 minutes of cooking. Bake for a total of 25 to 30 minutes, or until golden brown. Remove from the oven and let cool.

This is a great bread to conquer: once you have the hang of it, you can experiment in many different ways, changing the herbs inside and on top, for instance.

PANE CON I FICHI
Fig Bread

This is the breakfast bread I make at the cooking school, and it is very popular. We call it *panmarino*, the Italian equivalent of brioche. It's light, has a very yellow interior, is rich in flavor, and keeps well. It can be made into buns; bake these for 20 minutes only.

MAKES 2 LOAVES

12 ounces dried figs

juice and grated zest of 6 unwaxed oranges

½ ounce fresh yeast, or 2 teaspoons active dry

⅔ cup warm water

¾ cup plus 2 tablespoons unsalted butter

4 cups unbleached flour

1½ teaspoons sea salt

⅓ cup (2 ounces) whole almonds, toasted

2 eggs, beaten

confectioner's sugar for dusting

1 Soak the figs in the orange juice and zest overnight. Don't worry if there is not enough juice to cover them; they simply need to be moistened.

2 In a small bowl, dissolve the yeast in a little of the water, and allow to activate for about 10 minutes. In a large bowl, rub the butter into the flour, along with the salt.

3 Cut up the figs to the size of a thumbnail, and coarsely chop the almonds. Add both to the flour, along with any leftover orange juice and zest.

4 Add the yeast mixture, the beaten eggs and the remaining water. Stir with a wooden spoon until a soft and pliable dough forms. Knead on a flat, floured work surface for 10 minutes, until soft and springy. Return to a clean bowl, cover with a damp dishcloth and allow to rise for 3 hours. (The richer the mixture, the slower the rise.)

5 Punch down the dough and form into two rounds. Chafe each round (see page 170) for a few minutes, then set on a baking sheet, covered with a cloth, to rise for an hour.

6 Preheat the oven to 400°.

7 Bake the loaves for 35 minutes, until they are golden and sound hollow when you tap on the bottom. Cool on a wire rack and dust with confectioner's sugar.

Figs are very high in iron, potassium, calcium and zinc, and they are also laxative in action because of their high fiber content. You could use fresh figs, which is what we do at the school since we have so many fig trees there. But try different fillings: a mixture of walnuts and seedless black grapes is also good.

SCHIACCIATA DOLCE

Sweet Flatbread

In the tombs of the Etruscans, early inhabitants of Italy, are curious drawings of daily activities, including depictions of pasta making and bread making. One such ancient bread was *schiacciata*, a flatbread that today has many different versions, depending on the region of Italy. *Schiacciata* means "squashed" or "flattened." In Siena it is a flat Easter cake with confectioner's sugar on top; in Florence, an hour's drive away, it is a flat pizza with herbs and onions. This recipe, a much older version of *schiacciata*, is made with a batterlike dough and baked in a deepish rectangular baking sheet.

MAKES 1 LARGE LOAF

¾ cup plus 2 tablespoons warm water

½ ounce fresh yeast, or 2 teaspoons
   active dry

2½ cups unbleached flour

1 large egg, lightly beaten

⅔ cup unsalted butter, melted

3 tablespoons superfine sugar

1 tablespoon each unwaxed orange and
   lemon zests, grated

⅛ teaspoon powdered or crumbled
   saffron

1 tablespoon vanilla extract

confectioner's sugar for dusting

1   Pour all the water into a large mixing bowl. Add the yeast and stir to dissolve, then leave for 5 minutes to froth.

2   Gradually add the measured flour and mix with your hands until a ball of dough is formed. Knead the dough vigorously on a lightly floured surface.

3   Oil a bowl, add the dough and turn the dough in the oil to coat it. Cover the bowl and leave the dough to rise until doubled in size, about 1 hour.

4   Punch the dough down in the bowl, then add the egg and all but 2 tablespoons of the melted butter, the sugar, orange and lemon zests, saffron and vanilla. Use a wooden spoon to gently incorporate the ingredients. The dough will be very soft and sticky. Add more flour if necessary. Mix for 10 minutes.

5   Use 1 tablespoon of the remaining melted butter to grease a baking sheet with a lip, measuring approximately 12 by 10 inches. Pour the dough onto the baking sheet and use a spatula to smooth it out to the edges. Brush the remaining melted butter over the top. Let the dough rise in a warm place, covered, for about 1½ hours.

6   Preheat the oven to 400°.

7   Bake the bread for 20 to 25 minutes, or until nicely golden on top. Cool on a wire rack. Cut into squares and dust with confectioner's sugar.

The bread has a slightly sweet flavor and is perfect served warm for breakfast, or for tea. It keeps well for up to two days.

COPPIA FERRARESE
Enriched Bread Rolls

Ferrara is famous for its water, which is why the bread of this region is so good. I learned about this recipe while talking with a baker in the piazza one evening – he was insistent that this was the one and only true recipe (there are many imitations). Since few of us have access to Ferrara water, bottled Italian still water will do!

MAKES ABOUT 12 ROLLS

¼ ounce fresh yeast, or
   1 teaspoon active dry
¾ cup plus 2 tablespoons warm
   water
4½ cups unbleached flour

2 teaspoons sea salt
3 tablespoons *Biga* (page 165)
3 tablespoons olive oil
3 tablespoons semolina for
   sprinkling

1 In a small bowl, dissolve the yeast in some of the warm water.

2 In a large mixing bowl, combine the flour and salt. Make a well in the flour, add the *biga*, oil, yeast mixture and the rest of the water, and stir to form a soft, pliable dough.

3 Turn out onto a floured surface and knead for 8 minutes. Put the dough into a clean bowl, cover with a damp cloth and allow to double in size, for 1½ hours.

4 Punch down the dough and "chafe" for 6 minutes (see page 170).

5 Cut the dough into 12 pieces, and divide each piece of dough

into 2 strips no longer than 5 inches in length. Twist 2 together one turn to join them in the middle. Do the same with the remaining strips to make 12 cross-shaped rolls. Place on a semolina-sprinkled baking sheet, and allow to rise for 20 minutes.

6 Meanwhile, preheat the oven to 400°.

7 Fill a roasting pan with ice cubes and place on the floor of the oven; this will create valuable moisture for the rolls and help to give them a better color and crust. Bake the rolls for 15 to 20 minutes, or until golden. Cool on a wire rack, and enjoy.

There are several types of yeast available. You could use dried yeast instead of fresh: as a general rule, halve the quantity of fresh, as the dried is concentrated. It too needs to be activated in warm water. Some breads can use easy-blend yeast, which is activated in the flour when the liquid is added.

COLOMBA PASQUALE
Easter Dove Bread

Easter is a time of great celebration and holiday in Italy, much more so than Christmas. This bread – made in the shape of the dove of peace – is rich with ingredients that would have been denied during Lent, the 40 days leading up to Easter. It is eaten at breakfast time and is never cut, but broken into pieces and enjoyed with an espresso.

MAKES 2 "DOVE" LOAVES

Sponge
¾ cup milk
¾ ounce fresh yeast, or 3 teaspoons active
   dry
1 cup unbleached flour

Dough
3 large eggs
1 large egg yolk
½ cup superfine sugar
½ cup unsalted butter

½ teaspoon sea salt
1 teaspoon vanilla extract
1 teaspoon grated zest of unwaxed orange
2¾ cups unbleached flour
½ cup dark or golden seedless raisins, plus
   a few extra
½ cup mixed candied fruit

To finish
¾ cup (3½ ounces) split blanched almonds
confectioner's sugar for dusting

1 To make the sponge, heat the milk gently until lukewarm, then remove from the heat and whisk in the yeast. Stir in the flour, then cover with plastic wrap and allow to rest for 30 minutes.

2 To make the dough, whisk the eggs and egg yolk with the sugar. Melt the butter and, when cool, whisk it in. Stir in the salt, vanilla and orange zest, then add the flour.

3 Either by hand or with an electric mixer, beat the sponge into the dough mixture until it is smooth, about 2 minutes. Then add the ½ cup raisins and candied fruit. Place the dough in a buttered bowl, cover with plastic wrap and let rise until doubled in size, about 2 hours.

4 Punch the dough down and turn out onto a lightly floured surface. Divide into 4 equal pieces and form each piece into a torpedo

shape. Place one piece on top of another piece at right angles, at the center, to get a "dove" shape, with body and outstretched wings. Do the same with the remaining pieces to make another dove. Use the extra raisins for the eyes.

5 Place each dove on a separate baking sheet lined with parchment paper. Cover loosely and allow to rise again at room temperature until doubled in size, about 1 hour.

6 Preheat the oven to 375°.

7 Stud the dough shapes with the almonds to look like feathers – I usually do this at the wing tips – and bake for about 20 minutes, or until golden brown in color and firm to the touch. Cool on a wire rack, and then dust with confectioner's sugar.

The same recipe can be used to make the famous Italian Christmas bread, panettone.

PANE AL MIELE

Honey Bread

Miele, honey, has featured in cooking since the times of the Ancients. The Egyptians, Greeks and Romans all used it, not only as a sweetener, but also as a preservative. Apicius, the knowledgeable Roman gourmet, tells us that vegetables, herbs and fruit were preserved by covering them with a combination of honey and vinegar. Honey was also used in bread recipes and what were called "honey cakes," not so much for the sweetness it offered, but because it kept the bread fresh for longer. And indeed this bread does keep quite well.

MAKES 1 LOAF

½ **cup warm water**

½ **ounce fresh yeast, or 2 teaspoons active dry**

1 **cup plus 2 tablespoons warm whole milk**

¾ **cup plus 3 tablespoons clear honey**

2 **tablespoons melted unsalted butter, cooled**

2 **tablespoons extra virgin olive oil**

1 **large egg**

1 **tablespoon sea salt**

2 **tablespoons anise seeds**

1 **tablespoon grated zest of unwaxed lemon**

4 **cups unbleached flour**

⅓ **cup seedless raisins**

½ **cup (2 ounces) shelled walnuts**

⅓ **cup dried prunes, pitted and chopped**

1 Place the water in a large bowl, sprinkle with the yeast, and stir to dissolve. Let the mixture sit for 10 minutes, or until foamy.

2 Add the milk, ¾ cup honey, the butter, oil, egg, salt, anise seeds and lemon zest to the yeast, and stir the ingredients well.

3 Add the flour and mix with your hands to obtain a ball of dough. Add additional flour (if necessary) until you have a nonstick ball. Knead for 10 minutes to form a soft, elastic and smooth dough. Cover with a damp dishcloth in a bowl and let rise for 1½ hours, or until doubled in size.

4 In a small bowl combine the raisins, walnuts and prunes.

5 Punch down the dough and turn it out onto a floured surface. Knead for 2 to 3 minutes, then roll out into a 16-inch-diameter circle. With a brush spread 2 tablespoons of the remaining honey over the dough and sprinkle with three-quarters of the fruit and nut filling.

6 Roll the dough up to obtain a 16-inch-long loaf, 3 inches thick. Crimp the ends, or the honey will seep out. Place the roll on a lightly greased baking sheet and set aside, covered with a damp towel, for 30 minutes to rise.

7 Preheat the oven to 400°.

8 Bake the bread for 30 minutes, or until golden. Remove to a wire rack, and with a brush spread on the remaining tablespoon of honey and then sprinkle the remaining fruit and nut filling over the loaf. Cool completely before serving. Cut crosswise into slices and serve.

Do experiment with different types of honey. I love chestnut honey and thyme honey. Indulge in some local honey if you suffer from allergies or have a reaction to pollen when abroad, since this will help lessen the symptoms.

PANE DI SPINACI DELLA NONNA

Grandmother's Spinach Bread

The Italians eat lots of bread and are crazy about greens – and this recipe combines them both. It's the sort of thing they might eat at harvest time, as an all-in-one meal (the Italian equivalent of a pasty or pie). It would be a good bread to take on a picnic. It also keeps very well.

MAKES 1 LOAF

½ ounce fresh yeast, or 2 teaspoons active dry

2¼ cups warm water

3 cups unbleached flour

1¾ cups plus 2 tablespoons fine semolina flour

2 teaspoons sea salt

1 pound fresh spinach

2 tablespoons extra virgin olive oil

1 garlic clove, peeled and minced

2 tablespoons black olives, pitted and finely chopped

freshly ground black pepper

1 large egg white, beaten with 2 teaspoons water (egg wash)

a handful of sesame seeds

1 In a large bowl dissolve the yeast in ½ cup of the water. Let it sit, covered, for 10 minutes, until foamy.

2 Add the remaining water and stir well. Stir in the flour and semolina flour, tablespoon by tablespoon, along with the salt. Mix with your hands until a ball of dough is formed.

3 Knead vigorously for 10 minutes, then place in a lightly oiled bowl. Let stand for 1½ hours, covered, until doubled in size.

4 Meanwhile, prepare the filling. Wash and drain (but do not dry) the spinach thoroughly, discarding any really tough stems. Put the leaves into a pan without any additional water, cover, and cook over medium heat until wilted. Drain the spinach and allow it to cool. Squeeze out all the excess water, and then chop very finely.

5 In a frying pan, heat the olive oil, add the garlic, and sauté until soft. Add the chopped spinach and cook for 2 to 3 minutes, then add the olives and some pepper to taste. Remove from the heat and let cool completely.

6 When the dough has risen, punch it down and roll it into a circle about 16 inches in diameter. Lift the dough onto a greased baking sheet. Spoon on the spinach filling, and spread it to within 1 inch of the edges.

7 Roll the dough up tightly like a jelly roll. Turn the ends under to seal. Make random ½-inch-deep slits on the top with a knife. Brush the top of the dough with egg wash and sprinkle with sesame seeds. Cover with a towel and let the bread rise for 30 minutes.

8 Meanwhile, preheat the oven to 400°.

9 Bake the bread for 35 minutes, or until golden, then remove to a wire rack. Cool before serving. Slice on the diagonal to reveal the wonderful swirl of the filling.

Please feel free to change the ingredients in the middle. The spinach is traditional to Naples and its environs, but you could use cheese or other cooked vegetables, or a mixture.

TORTA AL TESTO

Bread of the Tile

The flat, crusty appearance of this age-old peasant bread inspired its name, *testo*, which means "tile" in Italian. *Torta al Testo* is found exclusively in its native Umbria and usually *a casa:* in the home.

MAKES 8 ROUNDS

½ ounce fresh yeast, or 2
    teaspoons active dry
2¼ cups plus 1 tablespoon
    warm water
4½ cups flour
1½ teaspoons salt
1 tablespoon olive oil

Filling

9 ounces fontina cheese
4½ ounces arugula
sea salt and freshly ground
    black pepper

1 In a small bowl, dissolve the yeast in a little of the water. Let stand for 5 minutes, then stir to dissolve. Combine the flour and salt in a large bowl. Make a well in the center and add the yeasted water and the oil. Mix in the flour and stir in the remaining water as needed to form a firm, moist dough.

2 Turn the dough out onto a lightly floured surface and knead until smooth, shiny and elastic, about 10 minutes.

3 Put the dough in a clean bowl and cover with a dishcloth. Allow to rise until doubled in size, about 30 minutes. Punch down, then let rest for 10 minutes.

4 Divide the dough into 8 pieces. On a lightly floured surface, roll out each piece of dough to form a round 8 inches across and ¼ inch thick. If the dough resists rolling out, allow it to rest for 1 to 2 minutes, then continue.

5 Heat a heavy frying pan or griddle over medium heat until very hot, about 10 minutes.

6 Place one of the dough rounds in the hot pan and prick all over with a fork to prevent air bubbles. Cook until golden on both sides, flipping it over frequently to avoid scorching and to aid even cooking. Repeat with the remaining dough rounds.

7 Stack the rounds on top of each other and cover with a dishcloth to keep soft. When cool, use a sharp knife to cut around the edge of each bread, and separate it into 2 halves. Preheat the oven to 400°.

8 Top one half of each bread with fontina and arugula and season with salt and pepper. Place the other half on top of the filling and place the stuffed breads on baking sheets. Bake until breads are hot and the cheese has melted. Cut into wedges and serve warm.

SCHIACCIATA DI UVA

Fresh Grape Flatbread

This sweet flatbread is best served warm. This delicious recipe is made to celebrate the grape harvest in Italy, which takes place in October. You can also use white grapes rather than red for variety.

MAKES 1 LARGE LOAF

Starter

½ ounce fresh yeast, or 2 teaspoons
    active dry

⅔ cup warm water

1 cup unbleached flour

Dough

½ ounce fresh yeast, or 2 teaspoons
    active dry

¾ cup warm water (105° to 115°)

3¼ cups unbleached flour

1½ teaspoons sea salt

3 tablespoons superfine sugar

3 tablespoons extra virgin olive oil

Filling and topping

1¼ cups seedless raisins

1 glass *vin santo* or sweet white wine

1 pound seedless red grapes

3 tablespoons Demerara sugar

1 handful fennel seeds for
    scattering on top

1 To make the starter, sprinkle the yeast into the ⅔ cup water. Stir to dissolve and let stand for 5 minutes.

2 Add the flour and mix to form a thick batter. Cover with a dishcloth and leave to ferment at room temperature for 12 to 36 hours, or until it forms a loose, bubbling batter.

3 To make the dough, sprinkle the yeast into ⅓ cup of the water and stir to dissolve.

4 Combine the flour and sea salt in a large bowl and add the sugar. Make a well in the center of the flour and pour in the yeasted water, the oil and the starter. Add the flour and stir in the remaining water to form a soft, sticky dough. Add additional water one tablespoon at a time, as necessary.

5 Turn out onto a lightly floured work surface and knead the dough for about 10 minutes, until smooth, silky and elastic in texture.

6 Put the dough in a lightly oiled bowl and cover with a dishcloth. Leave to rise for

1½ to 2 hours, or until doubled in size. Punch down and chafe for 5 minutes (see page 170), then let rest for about 10 minutes.

7 Divide the dough into 2 equal pieces. Roll out both pieces on a lightly floured work surface to form 2 rounds about 9½ inches in diameter. Place one of the rounds on a baking sheet that has been lightly oiled.

8 To make the filling, marinate the raisins in the wine for at least 2 hours, preferably overnight. Drain thoroughly and reserve the wine as a special treat for the baker! Spread the raisins evenly over one round of dough. Put the second round of dough on top and pinch the edges together.

9 Cover with a dishcloth and let rise until doubled in size, about 30 minutes. Preheat the oven to 400°.

10 Sprinkle with Demerara sugar and fennel seeds. Bake for approximately 45 minutes, or until the crust is golden. Cool on a wire rack.

FRUTTA E NOCI

In my family, and the families of most Italians, we eat seasonal fruit fresh from the tree or vine, usually at the end of a meal. This healthy practice is completely understandable, because Italian fruit is so good, its natural sweetness intensified by the long growing season with sunny days, and by rich soil and generations of farmers who truly understand the land. Most fruits contain a good proportion of vitamins and minerals, principally vitamins C, E and A (the latter in yellow and orange fruits).

After a winter spent eating apples, pears and a selection of preserved fruit – for fruit is traditionally dried and bottled as well – it is wonderful to look forward to the first fresh cherries, to be followed later by luscious sun-ripened peaches, apricots and figs. In my travels throughout the length and breadth of Italy, I have noticed that fruit forms one of the most striking features of the landscape: the groves of lemon and orange trees, for instance, the fruit shining like beacons among the intensely green leaves. Fruit is bought daily at the markets, if it is not grown in the garden at home, and it is also eaten daily. I have very fond memories of my grandfather sitting at the head of the table peeling fruit for my sisters and me, and feeding it to us as if we were baby birds.

Nuts, too, play a vital role in the Italian diet. They are a storehouse of energy in the form of protein and fat, and they are high in nutrients, primarily vitamins A, B, C, D and E, and the minerals calcium and magnesium. They are eaten and enjoyed fresh, mainly in the winter months, but they are used in various forms throughout the year, in myriad recipes. Nature has actually designed them to last a year, from one harvest to the next, but once out of their shells, they start to deteriorate and oxidize, their oils turning rancid. Any nuts, particularly those out of their shells, should be kept cool and away from strong sunlight; they should be bought from a reliable source and used as quickly as possible.

In Italy, the harvesting of fruit and nuts calls for many festivals. In Sicily, people celebrate the flowering of almond trees in February; elsewhere, the first cherries are formally welcomed in June; and the autumn heralds the chestnut season in the north of the country, when nuts are roasted in the embers of huge bonfires. A multitude of recipes from every region mark and show appreciation for the quality and quantity of fruit or nuts available locally, and I have gathered together an interesting selection. All of the dishes in this chapter are sweet, although nuts in particular are used in many savory recipes as well. (Think of pine nuts in pesto, chestnuts in vegetable bakes and walnuts in pasta sauces.) Many of the recipes given here are for little biscuits, *biscotti*, or pastries, which in Italy are eaten not as a dessert after lunch or dinner, but as a delicious addition to coffee in the morning or afternoon.

FICHI SECCHI IN VINO

Dried Figs in Wine

One of the best fruit desserts is simply a bowl of fresh figs. I only see them in the market occasionally outside Italy, and when I do I serve them at the end of a meal with a dollop of sweet creamy mascarpone on the side. For the times when fresh figs are not available, this is a wonderful family recipe that uses dried figs.

SERVES 4

12 large dried figs
1 cup (4 ounces) freshly shelled
  walnuts, chopped
½ cup dry red wine

4 tablespoons fragrant clear
  honey
1 tablespoon grated zest of
  unwaxed orange
mascarpone cheese, for serving
  (optional)

1 Preheat the oven to 350°. Lightly grease a deep 6-inch round casserole dish.

2 With your fingers, open each fig at the stem end to form a small hole. Stuff some of the walnuts into each fig, and then place, stem end up, in a single layer in the buttered casserole.

3 In a small saucepan, heat the wine and honey together, stirring until the honey dissolves. Pour the mixture over the figs. Sprinkle with the orange zest, cover the casserole tightly with a lid or foil, and bake for 30 minutes.

4 Let the figs cool to room temperature in the casserole. To serve, place 3 figs on each plate and drizzle with some of the wine sauce. Serve with mascarpone cheese, if desired.

Try to buy dried figs labeled "preservative-free," sold in health-food stores. Many dried fruits are coated with E 220, sulphur dioxide, which may preserve and soften the fruits but can provoke allergic reactions. When buying fresh figs, check that they are ripe. Smell each one: it should be very, very sweet and honey-fragrant. Then give it a gentle squeeze: it should just give to your fingertips. The color will depend on the variety.

TORRONE DI SESAMO

Sesame Nougat

Torrone is enjoyed throughout Italy at all times of the year, but it features particularly at festive occasions such as Christmas, New Year and *Carnevale*.

MAKES ABOUT 12 SMALL SQUARES

¾ cup plus 2 tablespoons fragrant clear honey

¼ cup superfine sugar

1½ cups (8 ounces) sesame seeds

1¼ cups (7 ounces) whole almonds, roasted and chopped

2 teaspoons almond or sunflower oil

1 In a saucepan, melt the honey gently, add the sugar, and slowly bring to a boil. Add the sesame seeds and almonds, and keep stirring over low heat until the mixture thickens.

2 Grease a baking sheet with the oil. Pour the mixture onto the baking sheet and flatten with an oiled rolling pin. Allow to cool a little.

3 Cut into small squares with a sharp knife, then let cool completely. Store in an airtight container.

Sesame seeds are about 50 percent highly unsaturated oil, and 20 to 25 percent protein. They are also rich in the B vitamins, calcium, phosphorus and iron. The seeds grow in a pod that pops open as it dries: hence the expression "Open sesame."

TORRONCINI

Nougat

Many different varieties of nougat are made throughout Italy. This one comes from Sicily and, once again, reveals the Arabic influence. Nougat is eaten as a *merenda*, a snack, at eleven in the morning, or four in the afternoon.

MAKES 18 LITTLE SQUARES

2¼ cups granulated sugar

¼ cup fragrant clear honey

1½ cups (9 ounces) almonds, toasted and chopped

2 cups (9 ounces) shelled pistachio nuts, chopped

1 Dissolve the sugar with the honey in a saucepan over low heat, then add the almonds and pistachios. Cook for 5 to 10 minutes to allow the flavors to blend.

2 Grease a slab of marble (or other cold heatproof surface) with a little vegetable oil. Pour the nougat onto the marble, spread out with a spatula to ¼ inch thick, and immediately cut into long strips and then into short lengths the size of a large postage stamp.

3 When the nougat is cold, wrap each piece in waxed paper, and store in an airtight container.

The fresher the nuts, the crunchier and more nutritious the torroncini *will be. Pistachio nuts have a unique flavor, and they are about 18 percent protein and 55 percent unsaturated oil. Pistachios and almonds are both great energy boosters.*

MINNI DI SANTA AGATA

Baked Sweet Pastries

These dome-shaped pastries are made from a sweet pasta dough. Their shape inspired the name, which, literally translated, means "breasts of Saint Agatha."

MAKES ABOUT 12 PASTRIES

Pastry

2 cups all-purpose or Italian "00" (soft wheat) flour

5 tablespoons superfine sugar

½ cup chilled unsalted butter, cut into pieces

1 egg

1 tablespoon finely grated zest of unwaxed lemon

a pinch of sea salt

Filling

1 tablespoon shelled hazelnuts, toasted

1 tablespoon candied orange peel or mixed citrus peel

1 ounce semisweet chocolate, with 50 percent cocoa solids

1 cup (8 ounces) ricotta cheese

¼ cup superfine sugar

1½ teaspoons vanilla extract

1 egg yolk

sifted confectioner's sugar and cocoa powder for dusting

1 To make the pastry dough, put the flour and sugar into a food processor and, processing at full speed, add the butter pieces gradually until well combined. With the food processor still running, add the egg, lemon zest and salt. Turn the dough onto waxed paper, flatten, cover and chill in the fridge for 30 minutes. Allow it to return to room temperature before rolling.

2 For the filling, finely chop the hazelnuts and orange peel, and grate the chocolate. Push the ricotta through a sieve into a bowl. Stir in the sugar, vanilla, egg yolk, hazelnuts, peel and chocolate until combined.

3 Preheat the oven to 350°. Grease a large baking sheet.

4 Roll out the pastry to about ¼ inch thick. Cut into circles with a 1¼-inch cutter. Put 2 teaspoons filling on a pastry circle and top with another pastry circle. Press the edges to seal all around. Place on the baking sheet and prick the top of each with a fork.

5 Bake the pastries for 20 minutes, or until golden. Let cool, then dredge with confectioner's sugar and cocoa powder.

During a recent teaching trip in Italy, representatives of a major supermarket chain, who were attending, became very excited by this recipe, feeling it could be marketed as an Italian version of our Christmas mince pie. It certainly has as much diversity in its flavor and, in fact, tastes divine!

TORTA DI NOCE

Walnut Tart

Best served with a small glass of *vin santo*, perfect for breakfast in the morning (if you like a little alcohol then, as many Italians do), or for *merenda*, a little coffee break. The pastry is foolproof, wonderfully easy to handle, and can be used in many other recipes.

SERVES 4 TO 6

1 cup butter

3¾ cups Italian "00" (soft wheat) or
   cake (not self-rising) flour

1 cup superfine sugar

4 large egg yolks

2 cups (8 ounces) fresh
   walnut halves

¾ cup (6 ounces) apricot conserve

sifted confectioner's sugar
   for dusting

1 To make the pastry, rub the butter into the flour until the mixture is the consistency of breadcrumbs. Stir in the sugar, then add the egg yolks, and mix with your hands to form a moist, crumbly dough. Wrap in plastic wrap and refrigerate for 1 hour.

2 Remove the dough from the refrigerator. Allow the dough an hour to return to room temperature before you roll it out. During this hour, preheat the oven to 375°.

3 Roast the walnut halves on a baking sheet in the oven for 7 minutes, or until only just golden. When cool, roughly chop them.

4 Divide the dough in two. Place half the dough between two sheets of floured plastic wrap, and shape it into a 12-by-16-inch rectangle, using the tips of your fingers and quick, light movements. Shape the second half of the dough to the same size in the same way. Slip one dough rectangle onto an oblong baking sheet (about 16 by 12 inches), using the plastic wrap to help you transport the dough. Remove the plastic wrap.

5 Spread a thick layer of apricot conserve right to the edges of this square, then sprinkle half the walnuts all over the top. Cover this layer with the second sheet of dough. Do not seal.

6 Bake in the middle of the oven for 30 minutes, or until the top is golden brown.

7 Remove from the oven and reduce the temperature to 325°. Push the remaining walnut pieces evenly on and over the still-soft pastry top. Put the tart back into the oven for 10 minutes more.

8 Cut into small squares and let cool. Serve dredged with confectioner's sugar.

You could show ingenuity and use different nuts: hazelnuts and almonds work well together. This is a very classic dish from Minori, my village: you go into the local pasticceria, buy a small square in a paper napkin, and enjoy it standing at the bar with a rich espresso. The sweetness of the tart perfectly balances the bitterness of the coffee.

PAN ROZZO

Spiced Almond and Chocolate Cake

This is dedicated to almond and chocolate lovers. It is a specialty of the Abruzzi e Molise, an area on the east coast of Italy, which produces magnificent almonds.

SERVES 6

⅔ cup Italian "00" (soft wheat) or cake (not self-rising) flour

⅓ cup potato starch flour

a pinch of ground cinnamon

4 eggs, separated

⅓ cup superfine sugar

⅓ cup (2 ounces) ground almonds

3 tablespoons unsalted butter, melted

2 tablespoons Amaretto di Saronno (almond liqueur)

3 ounces semisweet chocolate, with 70 percent cocoa solids, broken into pieces

1 tablespoon water

1 Preheat the oven to 350°. Grease and line with waxed paper a 7-inch round cake pan.

2 Sift the two flours together with the cinnamon. Put the egg yolks in a separate mixing bowl with the sugar and whisk until light and frothy. Fold in the flours and the almonds, along with the melted butter and liqueur.

3 Beat the egg whites until stiff, then carefully fold into the mixture. Spoon the batter into the prepared pan, and smooth the surface.

4 Bake for about 1 hour, or until well risen. Transfer the pan to a wire rack to cool, then turn the cake out of the pan.

5 Melt the chocolate with the water in a double boiler or in a metal bowl over a pan of simmering water. Spread over the cake to cover it completely. Allow the chocolate to set before serving.

Potato starch flour gives a magnificent light texture to the cake. Buy it from health-food stores. It consists of the pure starch gathered after soaking grated or pulped potatoes in water, and it can be very useful for those on a gluten-free diet.

ZUCCOTTO

"Little Pumpkin"

This traditional Tuscan dessert is easily recognized because of the icing sugar and cocoa with which it is always dusted. The recipe calls for Italian sponge cake, which is known as *pan di spagna*. It's like a small pumpkin in shape, thus its name.

SERVES 8

Sponge

6 eggs, separated

1¼ cups confectioner's sugar, sifted

1 teaspoon clear honey

1 teaspoon vanilla extract

½ cup potato starch flour, sifted

Filling

½ cup (3 ounces) shelled almonds, toasted and chopped

⅔ cup (3 ounces) shelled hazelnuts, toasted and chopped

11 ounces semisweet chocolate, half of it chopped, and half melted

4¼ cups heavy cream, whipped

To serve

3 tablespoons rum

3 tablespoons brandy

3 tablespoons cherry brandy

2 tablespoons confectioner's sugar, sifted

2 tablespoons good cocoa powder, sifted

1 First make the sponge cake. Butter and flour a 10-inch round cake pan. Preheat the oven to 375°.

2 Put the egg yolks in a mixing bowl with the confectioner's sugar, honey and vanilla. Beat vigorously with a whisk until foaming and pale yellow. In a separate bowl beat the egg whites until stiff, and fold into the egg-yolk mixture. Then sift in the potato starch flour and fold very delicately into the mixture.

3 Pour into the prepared cake pan and bake for 40 minutes.

4 Remove from the oven and ease out of the pan onto a wire rack. Let cool.

4 Now for the filling. Stir the almonds, hazelnuts and chopped chocolate into the whipped cream. Divide this mixture in half and stir the melted chocolate into one half. Refrigerate both cream mixtures until just before use.

5 When the cake is cool, slice the crust off the top and cut the cake in half horizontally. Put one half away to use another time.

6 Combine the rum and brandies and brush the sponge with the alcohol until pliable. Place it in a 1-quart pudding basin, and gently ease it down to take the shape of the base of the bowl.

7 Pile in one of the cream mixtures and smooth the top, then pile on the second cream mixture. Smooth the top. Set aside to soak for about 1 hour.

8 Invert the set "pumpkin" onto a serving plate, and dust with confectioner's sugar and cocoa powder.

When you toast nuts, you diminish their nutritional value by about a third, but toasting does enhance the flavor of the nuts.

FIORENTINI

Italian Florentines

There are many variations on this luxurious biscuit, which is said to have originated in Austria, despite its Italian-sounding name.

MAKES 8 PIECES

1 cup (5½ ounces) whole blanched almonds

1¼ cups (5½ ounces) whole blanched hazelnuts

8 ounces natural red candied cherries

3½ ounces candied fruits (such as melon, lemon, orange)

½ cup all-purpose flour

½ teaspoon ground allspice

½ teaspoon freshly grated nutmeg

½ cup superfine sugar

½ cup clear honey

4 ounces semisweet chocolate

1 Preheat the oven to 350°. Grease a 9-inch round cake pan, and line it with baking parchment.

2 Put the almonds and hazelnuts on a baking sheet, and toast in the oven for 10 minutes. Put in a mixing bowl, and allow to cool.

3 Wash the cherries, then chop all the fruits and add to the nuts. Sift the flour, allspice and nutmeg over the fruits and nuts, and stir to combine.

4 In a saucepan, warm the sugar and honey together over low heat until the sugar has dissolved. Add the honey mixture to the fruit mixture, and stir together.

5 Transfer the mixture to the prepared pan, and level the top. Bake for 25 minutes. Allow to cool in the pan.

6 Break the chocolate into small pieces and melt in a double boiler. Evenly spread the chocolate over the nut mixture. When set, cut into serving pieces.

Buy candied fruits whole rather than in pieces. These are a real delicacy in Italy, and some of the best candied fruits come from there. They take ages to make, since it's a very delicate operation, so be prepared for their high price.

TORTA ALLE SUSINE E NOCCIOLE

Warm Plum and Hazelnut Cake

Fresh, juicy plums, which in Italy are ripe in mid-September, give this cake a wonderfully moist texture. It is best eaten warm, with a big dollop of whipped cream or crème fraîche.

SERVES 6

1 pound ripe plums
½ cup unsalted butter
⅓ cup packed brown sugar
2 large eggs
2 cups self-rising flour, sifted

½ cup (2 ounces) hazelnuts, chopped
sifted confectioner's sugar for dusting

1 Preheat the oven to 375°. Grease an 8-inch round cake pan, and line with parchment paper.

2 Cut the plums into quarters, discarding the stones.

3 Cream together the butter and sugar until light and fluffy. Then beat in the eggs one at a time, and fold in the flour.

4 Carefully fold in the plums and then pile the mixture into the prepared pan. Sprinkle the hazelnuts on the top, and bake for 45 to 50 minutes, or until golden brown and firm to the touch.

5 Allow to cool slightly in the pan, then turn out onto a plate and serve slightly warm, dusted with confectioner's sugar.

If fresh plums are not available, you can substitute other fruits, such as pears, apples or raspberries, but use only ripe fruit that is in season and bursting with flavor.

TORTA DI CILIEGIA
Succulent Cherry Cake

My great friend in Verona gave me this recipe, which is made to celebrate the new season's cherries in May and June. You have to be quick when harvesting cherries, otherwise the birds get them. There are many varieties, but the best are said to be from Ravenna, near Bologna. Displays of cherries in markets are labeled with their area of origin, and the cherries are also sold in various labeled stages of maturity: ripe, nearly ripe, etc.

SERVES 6

½ cup unsalted butter, softened

⅔ cup superfine sugar

4 eggs, separated

2 cups Italian "00" (soft wheat) or cake (not self-rising) flour

1 teaspoon baking powder

1 tablespoon brandy

a pinch of sea salt

1 pound 6 ounces fresh cherries, washed and pitted

sifted confectioner's sugar for dusting

1 Preheat the oven to 350°. Grease and flour an 8-inch cake pan.

2 In a large mixing bowl, cream the butter and sugar together until light and fluffy. In a separate bowl, beat the egg yolks with a little of the flour. Sift the remaining flour with the baking powder, and carefully fold into the creamed mixture along with the egg yolks and brandy.

3 Whisk the egg whites with the salt until they stand in stiff peaks. Add 3 teaspoons of the whisked egg white to the creamed mixture and stir until blended. Fold in the remaining egg white with a metal spoon and carefully spoon the batter into the prepared pan.

4 Scatter the cherries over the top of the batter and press them down lightly. Bake for 35 to 40 minutes, or until the cake is well risen and firm to the touch.

5 Allow the cake to cool in the pan, then turn out onto a wire rack and dust with confectioner's sugar.

A hand-held cherry pitter speeds up the work of pitting cherries, and olives as well. I have many happy memories of sitting under the vines with friends, passatempo, *pitting cherries.*

TORTA DI PESCHE SECCHE E LIMONE

Peach and Lemon Tart

The intensity of the peach works beautifully with the lemon in this recipe, which came from my aunt in Minori. When there is a glut of peaches, in August, she halves them, cuts out the stone, and lays them on a board in the sun, covered with muslin to keep the flies away. The sun is very intense at that time of year, especially at midday, so the peach halves can dry in as short a time as 3 hours.

SERVES 8

Pastry

2⅓ cups Italian "00" (soft wheat) or
   cake (not self-rising) flour
¾ cup confectioner's sugar
½ cup unsalted butter
1 large egg
a pinch of sea salt
a few drops of vanilla extract
zest of 1 unwaxed lemon, grated

Filling

1⅓ cups (8 ounces) dried peaches
3 tablespoons water
juice and grated zest of 4 unwaxed
   lemons
½ cup unsalted butter
1 tablespoon granulated sugar
4 eggs, lightly beaten
whipped cream for garnishing
   (optional)

1 To make the pastry, sift the flour and confectioner's sugar into a mixing bowl, and rub in the butter until the mixture resembles breadcrumbs. Make a well in the center, and add the egg, salt, vanilla and lemon zest. Gradually work the flour in from the edges and blend to a smooth dough. Wrap in plastic wrap and let rest in the fridge for about 30 minutes before using.

2 Preheat the oven to 400°. Meanwhile, in a saucepan, boil the dried peaches in the water until they soften, about 20 minutes. Drain and purée the peaches.

3 To make the filling, in a double boiler or a metal bowl over a pan of gently simmering water, combine the lemon juice and zest, butter and sugar. Stir

with a wooden spoon until the butter melts. Stir in the eggs, and cook over medium to low heat until the filling thickens enough to coat the back of the spoon. Be careful not to let the mixture curdle. Remove from the heat and leave to cool.

4 Roll out the pastry to line a 9-inch tart pan with a removable base. Line the interior of the pastry shell with parchment paper and fill with pie weights or dried beans. Bake for 10 minutes, or until nicely golden.

5 Remove the weights and paper, and pour the lemon filling into the pastry shell in an even layer. Spread the puréed peaches on top.

6 Chill for 1 hour, and serve, with whipped cream if desired.

When fruit is dried, it becomes more intense in flavor, and its nutrients are virtually doubled in the sense of weight: a prune contains more nutrients per ounce than does the original plum. The sugar content obviously becomes very concentrated as well, but because this is natural, it is not harmful.

BRUTTI MA BUONI

"Ugly but Good" Nutty Meringues

In Italy we eat a lot of small cakes or biscuits, particularly after the siesta to give us a burst of energy. Often they are taken to a friend's house and shared over a cup of coffee and lots of gossip. Wrapped in colored cellophane, they make wonderful presents.

MAKES ABOUT 18 MERINGUES

4 egg whites

¼ cup vanilla sugar (see below)

¼ cup (1¼ ounces) whole almonds, toasted

¼ cup (1¼ ounces) whole hazelnuts, toasted

1 Preheat the oven to 225°. Line a baking sheet with parchment paper.

2 Whisk the egg whites until stiff, gradually adding the sugar. Never add the sugar all at once, because the egg white mixture would collapse.

3 Coarsely chop the nuts, and fold them carefully into the meringue mixture.

4 Spoon 2 teaspoons for each meringue onto the parchment-lined baking sheet, and bake for 1½ hours, or until you get little crisp mounds.

5 Let the meringues cool, then store them in an airtight container.

Vanilla sugar can be made by burying a vanilla pod in a container of granulated or superfine sugar. I score the outside of the pod first to release as much of the essential oil as possible. As you use the sugar up, simply add more unflavored sugar to the container.

TORTA DI MASCARPONE

Lemon Mascarpone Cheesecake

This easy dessert can be served with fresh fruit such as raspberries or strawberries, when they are in season.

SERVES 6 TO 8

6 tablespoons unsalted butter

6 ounces amaretti biscuits

14 ounces mascarpone cheese

grated zest of 3 unwaxed lemons

juice of 1 lemon

½ cup superfine sugar

2 eggs, separated

2 tablespoons cornstarch

a pinch of salt

1 Preheat the oven to 350°.

2 Grease a deep 8-inch springform cake pan.

3 Melt the butter. Crush the biscuits, then stir them into the melted butter. Press into the bottom of the cake pan.

4 Put the mascarpone, lemon zest and juice, sugar and egg yolks in a bowl and stir together with a wooden spoon. Sprinkle the cornstarch over the top and fold in.

5 In a separate bowl, whisk the egg whites with the salt until stiff. Fold gently into the cheese mixture. Spread the mixture evenly in the cake pan and smooth the top.

6 Bake for 35 minutes, or until firm to the touch. Leave to cool in the pan.

This cheesecake can also be made with ricotta cheese, instead of mascarpone.

RICCIARELLI

Tuscan Almond Biscuits

The Sienese version of amaretti, the perfect *ricciarello* is crisp and powdery on the outside, and tender and moist inside.

MAKES ABOUT 16 BISCUITS

1 cup (6 ounces) whole blanched almonds, or 6 ounces ground almonds

2 egg whites

2 tablespoons all-purpose flour, sifted

⅛ teaspoon baking powder

1 cup confectioner's sugar, sifted, plus extra for rolling and dredging

3 drops almond extract

1 Preheat the oven to 425°.

2 If using whole almonds, roast them until golden – a few minutes only – then grind to a powder when they have cooled.

3 Beat the egg whites until they are stiff. Combine the flour and baking powder, and fold them into the egg whites. Fold in the 1 cup confectioner's sugar, the ground almonds and the almond extract to make a soft paste.

4 Pile some extra sugar onto a work surface. For each biscuit, roll a heaping teaspoon of the paste in the confectioner's sugar, then press it into an oblong shape, using the palm of your hand.

5 Place the biscuits well apart from each other on a thoroughly greased baking sheet. Bake for 10 to 12 minutes, or until the biscuits are pale and golden and slightly cracked, but with the insides still soft.

6 Let cool on the baking sheet. When cool, dredge with more confectioner's sugar.

Using fresh nuts is important for flavor, texture and maximum nutrients. Buy from a reliable source, and look for the date stamp.

213

BUCCELLATO PALERMITANO

Sweet Fig and Nut Cake

This rich Sicilian fruit and nut tart once more illustrates the Sicilian love of nuts and fruits. Every Sicilian market is full of stalls laden with the local fruits and nuts, and the ground on market days crunches underfoot with shells of the pistachios and pumpkin seeds the stallholders and their customers have enjoyed during the day. I have often thought it is this passion for nuts and seeds, with their vitamin E content, that makes the skin of Sicilians so healthy and fresh-looking.

SERVES 8

Pastry

⅔ cup unsalted butter

½ cup superfine sugar

3¼ cups Italian "00" (soft wheat) or cake (not self-rising) flour

¼ cup Marsala

a pinch of sea salt

1 egg yolk

½ cup (2 ounces) shelled pistachio nuts, finely chopped

confectioner's sugar, sifted

Filling

2 cups (11 ounces) chopped dried figs

2 cups (11 ounces) seedless raisins

½ cup (3½ ounces) shelled almonds, toasted and chopped

½ cup (2 ounces) shelled walnuts, chopped

grated zest of 2 unwaxed lemons

3½ ounces semisweet chocolate, with 70 percent cocoa solids, chopped

¼ cup Marsala

a pinch of ground cinnamon

1 To make the pastry, work the butter with the sugar and flour in a bowl together with the Marsala and salt. When you have a smooth dough, wrap it in plastic wrap and leave it to rest for an hour.

2 Make the filling by putting all the prepared ingredients into a saucepan. Simmer over low heat for 20 minutes, stirring frequently. Let cool.

3 Preheat the oven to 400°.

4 Using a rolling pin, roll the pastry dough into a rectangle about ½ inch thick. Pour the cooled filling into the center, roll up the dough, and join the ends to make a ring. Pierce the surface with a fork, place on a greased baking sheet and bake for 25 to 35 minutes, or until golden.

5 Beat the egg yolk. Brush the surface of the cake with the yolk, then sprinkle with the pistachio nuts and return to the oven for 5 minutes.

6 Place on a wire rack and let cool. Sprinkle with confectioner's sugar and serve.

Marsala is a fortified wine made in Sicily, one of the most famous Italian wines. There are many types – dry, semi-dry, sweet, gold, amber and ruby – and they are aged in wood for various times. For this cake, choose an old, dry wine.

TORTA DI MELE D'MARIA
Apple Cake

Maria, who owns San Orsola, the cooking school in Marschiano near Perugia where I've spent many happy years teaching, loves this apple cake. The soured cream adds a wonderful acidity to the sweetness of the apple.

SERVES 6 TO 8

1 tablespoon Demerara sugar
½ cup unsalted butter
½ cup superfine sugar
2 large eggs, separated
2 drops pure vanilla extract
¾ cup (4½ ounces) ground almonds

½ cup self-rising flour
⅔ cup sour cream
6 ounces Pippin or other tart apples
whipped cream for serving

1 Preheat the oven to 350°. Grease and line a 8-inch round cake pan with paper parchment, then sprinkle with the Demerara sugar.

2 Cream together the butter and sugar until light and fluffy. Beat in the egg yolks and vanilla, then fold in the almonds, flour and sour cream.

3 Whisk the egg whites until they hold their shape and then, using a metal spoon, fold into the creamed mixture.

4 Peel, core and slice the apples, and arrange them in the base of the prepared pan. Spoon the creamed mixture over the apples and smooth the surface. Bake for 45 to 60 minutes until golden and firm to the touch.

5 Invert on to a warmed serving plate, and serve warm with whipped cream.

Do experiment with other fruits: I've made this cake with soft fruits – with blackberries as well as apple when there was a glut of both – and with plums. The plums were fantastic!

215

PANFORTE DI SIENA

"Strong Bread"

This flat, sweet cake, which has a nougat-like texture, is rich in candied peel, toasted nuts and spices. It is a specialty of Siena, dating from the twelfth century. There are many variations, but this is my favorite, and it is said to be the original. There is a shop in Siena called Nannini that sells at least 15 different varieties of *panforte*; you can mix and match to decide which you like the best!

SERVES ABOUT 10

⅔ **cup (3 ounces) shelled hazelnuts**

½ **cup (3 ounces) blanched almonds, coarsely chopped**

1 **cup candied citrus peel, finely chopped**

¼ **cup cocoa powder**

½ **cup all-purpose flour**

½ **teaspoons ground cinnamon**

¼ **teaspoon ground mixed spice (cinnamon, cloves and nutmeg)**

½ **cup superfine sugar**

½ **cup clear honey**

Topping

2 **tablespoons confectioner's sugar**

1 **teaspoon ground cinnamon**

1 Preheat the oven to 300°.

2 Place the nuts in a bowl with the candied citrus peel, cocoa, flour and spices and stir until combined.

3 Put the sugar and honey in a pan and heat gently until a candy thermometer registers about 240°, or until a little of the mixture dropped into a cup of cool water forms a ball. Remove from the heat immediately, add to the nut mixture and stir until blended.

4 Transfer mixture to an 8-inch flan ring lined with nonstick parchment set on a baking sheet. Spread the mixture flat in the ring, making sure that it is no more than ½ inch thick.

5 Bake for 30 minutes. Turn on to a wire rack, peel off the paper and let cool.

6 Sprinkle the top thickly with sifted confectioner's sugar and cinnamon. Cut into small wedges.

The cake is said to have been devised during the Italian Crusades as something to give strength and energy, since nuts and seeds, the cocoa and honey are all storehouses of energy-giving nutrients.

NEPITELLA

Fig and Nut Pastries

I can't think of a nicer combination than figs and walnuts. Both are really health- and energy-giving foods. Eat these little half-moon, or *mezzaluna*, pastries with coffee or after a siesta, but never after lunch as a dessert.

MAKES ABOUT 14 PASTRIES

4 cups Italian "00" (soft wheat) or cake (not self-rising) flour

⅔ cup superfine sugar

⅔ cup butter, softened and cut into small pieces

3 eggs, 1 of them separated

a pinch of sea salt

Filling

2 cups (11 ounces) dried figs

1¼ cups (5½ ounces) shelled walnuts, ground

1 cup (5½ ounces) blanched almonds, toasted and ground

⅔ cup (3½ ounces) seedless raisins, soaked in lukewarm water for 15 minutes and drained

1 cup marmalade

finely grated zest of 3 unwaxed oranges

¼ teaspoon ground cloves

1 teaspoon ground cinnamon

1 Preheat the oven to 325°.

2 To make the pastry, sift the flour into a bowl, stir in the sugar and make a well in the center. Add the butter, 2 eggs, the separated egg yolk and the salt. Work the ingredients together with your fingertips to form a soft dough, then knead well until smooth and elastic. Shape the dough into a ball, cover with plastic wrap and chill.

3 Cook the figs in boiling water for 10 minutes. Drain thoroughly, cool, then chop. Place in a bowl with the other filling ingredients and stir until combined.

4 Using a rolling pin, roll the dough out to a sheet about ¼ inch thick. Cut into 4-inch circles, using a pastry cutter.

5 Put a little filling in the middle of each circle, then fold the dough over to form a half-moon shape. In a bowl, beat the egg white. Moisten the edges with the egg white, then press firmly to seal. Make a few cuts in the top of each pastry. Place on a greased baking sheet.

6 Bake for 25 to 35 minutes, or until golden. Serve hot or cold.

Nuts are a rich source of unsaturated oil and protein: almonds contain 40 to 60 percent of the former, 20 percent of the latter; walnuts 70 and 15 percent, respectively.

THE ITALIAN PANTRY

A WELL-STOCKED PANTRY, refrigerator and freezer not only save you endless shopping trips but also mean you are able to make a nutritious meal at a moment's notice. The following are the ingredients that I consider essential.

Pasta and Grains Grains of all sorts are useful sources of protein and carbohydrate. Pasta is made from wheat. I keep a large variety of dried pasta in various shapes and sizes. It should be an integral part of our lives, being economical, nutritious, quick to prepare, versatile and filling. When buying pasta, check the package to see that it is made from 100 percent durum wheat or states *"semola di grano."* When it contains egg it will also state *"all'uovo."* Check the date marking on the package to ensure freshness. Choice is very much based on personal taste, but as a general rule, use thin pasta for fairly thick sauces, hollow or twisted shapes for chunky sauces, wide, flat noodles for rich sauces and delicate shapes for light sauces. Tiny shapes are useful for soups. Store in airtight containers in a cool dark place.

Other useful grain foods are Italian "00" flour for making fresh pasta; unbleached flour for making bread; all-purpose white flour for cakes, pastries and sauces; Arborio, Carnaroli and Vialone Nano rices for risotto; Scotch barley; semolina.

Legumes Legumes are the seeds of plants, so they are rich in nutrients, particularly slow-release carbohydrates and vegetable protein. Those I use most include cannellini, haricot and *borlotti* (cranberry) beans (preferably dried); chickpeas; green lentils.

Nuts and Seeds A very rich source of natural fats and proteins for vegetarians. The ones I like best are hazelnuts; pine nuts; ground, flaked and blanched whole almonds; pistachio nuts; walnuts; chestnuts (dried); sesame seeds; pumpkin seeds; anise seeds; sunflower seeds. (Store in the refrigerator or freezer to preserve their vitamin E content.)

Dried Fruits Concentrated goodness! If possible choose those not preserved with sulphur dioxide, since they have more flavor and nutritional value: apricots; prunes; figs; pears; peaches; raisins; candied cherries; candied fruit.

Oils Cold-pressed olive oil, which is monounsaturated, is thought to contribute in a very positive way to the diet. Choose extra virgin olive oil for dressings and drizzling, olive oil for frying.

Cans Tomatoes (whole plum, and chopped); different sorts of beans, chickpeas, lentils (for use when you haven't time to soak dried).

Bottles and Jars Balsamic vinegar; red and white wine vinegar; green and black olives; capers (bottled in brine or vinegar, and salted); sun-dried tomatoes; *passata* (sieved tomatoes); gherkins; natural vanilla and almond extracts; honey; jams and preserves; red and white wine; a selection of spirits and liqueurs.

Herbs   Fresh herbs have a much better, truer flavor than dried herbs, and their nutritional benefits, contained in their essential oils, are still intact. Most can be easily grown on a windowsill, inside or out, or in the garden. Keep some dried or frozen herbs such as bay leaves, rosemary, oregano, sage and thyme for emergencies. Garlic, although not a herb (a member of the onion family), is used as a flavoring ingredient in the same way as fresh herbs. It will keep in a cool place for about six weeks.

Spices Whole fresh spices have better flavor than those bought ground. Buy whole spices and grind them yourself or, if buying ground, do so in small quantities and use them up quickly, because the essential oils that provide the flavor are quickly lost. Spices I find invaluable are whole nutmeg; whole and ground cinnamon and cloves (these are difficult to grind at home); powdered saffron; dried red pepper flakes; ground allspice and mixed spice (cinnamon, cloves and nutmeg) ; and fennel seeds. I also could not cook

without sea salt (coarse and flake varieties) and whole black peppercorns. For good flavor I use small fresh peppers (*peperoncino*).

Dairy Products These are a vital source of protein and fat for vegetarians. Such "pantry" ingredients are, of course, perishable and should therefore be stored in the refrigerator: free-range eggs, milk, light and heavy cream, sour cream, unsalted butter, and cheeses.

Parmesan This, the king of Italian cheese, is irreplaceable in Italian cooking: choose the expensive Parmigiano Reggiano or the slightly cheaper (because less matured) Grana Padano. Other Italian cheeses I find very useful in various dishes are pecorino, fontina, mozzarella, Dolcelatte, Gorgonzola, ricotta and mascarpone. These are usually made with animal rennet and therefore are not suitable for the strict vegetarian. However, the range of cheeses available made with vegetable rennet – including Parmesan – is increasing, so look out for them if this is important to you.

Miscellaneous Fresh and dried yeast; dried porcini (*Boletus edulis*, cèpe or wild mushroom); semisweet chocolate; sugars (keep a vanilla pod in superfine sugar for vanilla sugar); baking powder; cocoa powder; potato starch flour.

INDEX

223

ACKNOWLEDGEMENTS

What a joy to write this book and have the finest support available to make it happen.

Special thanks must go to my editor Susan Fleming for her constant good spirits and dedicated hard work. I had such fun with her and lots of giggles during the summer of 1998; to Margaret Little for shaping, developing and overseeing the whole project with gentle guidance and calm and for her ability to make the book stand out in the crowd; to Gaye Allen for her splendid designer's eye in ensuring the book looks so great, and for her kindness, gentleness and dedication throughout – working with you in Italy was wonderful; and to Jason Lowe for his exceptional photography – I adore the way in which he works, it was so inspiring and determined.